PRINT QUALITY TEST
For Self-Published Authors & Low-Content Creators

COMPARE THE PRINT QUALITY OF DIFFERENT FONTS, LINES, COVER COLORS, SHADES OF GRAY, DOTS, GRADIENTS & MORE

©2019 Winters Creative LLC
All rights reserved.

TABLE OF CONTENTS

LINES

Solid 6
Thin-Thin 8
Thick-Thick 10
Thin-Thick 12
Thick-Thin 14
Triple 16
Thick-Thin-Thick 18
Thin-Thick-Thin 20
White Diamonds 22
Japanese Dots 24
Dotted 26
Dashed 28
Dashed (3 & 2) 30
Dashed (4 & 4) 32
Straight Hash 34
Left Slant Hash 36
Right Slant Hash 38
Wavy 40

FONTS

Adobe Garamond Pro 44
Baskerville 48
Courier 52
Didot 56
Palatino 60
Times New Roman 64
Arial 68
Avenir Next 72
Brandon Grotesque 76
Futura 80
Helvetica Neue 84
Myriad Pro 88
Verdana 92

DOTS & DOT GRIDS

Black 98
Gray 99

OPACITY, GRADIENTS & PHOTOS

Opacity & Gradients 104
Photos 105

NOTES:

FOR REFERENCE
Trim Size: 6 x 9 inches
Page Count: 110
Paper: White
Cover: Matte

LINES

SOLID

0.25 pt

0.5 pt

0.75 pt

1 pt

1.5 pt

2 pt

2.5 pt

3 pt

4 pt

5 pt

6 pt

7 pt

8 pt

9 pt

10 pt

All lines featured in this section are standard Adobe InDesign strokes

Black: 75% Tint HEX #636466	Black: 50% Tint HEX #939598	Black: 25% Tint HEX #C7C8CA	Black: 10% Tint HEX #E6E7E8
0.25 pt	0.25 pt	0.25 pt	0.25 pt
0.5 pt	0.5 pt	0.5 pt	0.5 pt
0.75 pt	0.75 pt	0.75 pt	0.75 pt
1 pt	1 pt	1 pt	1 pt
1.5 pt	1.5 pt	1.5 pt	1.5 pt
2 pt	2 pt	2 pt	2 pt
2.5 pt	2.5 pt	2.5 pt	2.5 pt
3 pt	3 pt	3 pt	3 pt
4 pt	4 pt	4 pt	4 pt
5 pt	5 pt	5 pt	5 pt
6 pt	6 pt	6 pt	6 pt
7 pt	7 pt	7 pt	7 pt
8 pt	8 pt	8 pt	8 pt
9 pt	9 pt	9 pt	9 pt
10 pt	10 pt	10 pt	10 pt

THIN-THIN

0.25 pt

0.5 pt

0.75 pt

1 pt

1.5 pt

2 pt

2.5 pt

3 pt

4 pt

5 pt

6 pt

7 pt

8 pt

9 pt

10 pt

Black: 75% Tint HEX #636466	Black: 50% Tint HEX #939598	Black: 25% Tint HEX #C7C8CA	Black: 10% Tint HEX #E6E7E8
0.25 pt	0.25 pt	0.25 pt	0.25 pt
0.5 pt	0.5 pt	0.5 pt	0.5 pt
0.75 pt	0.75 pt	0.75 pt	0.75 pt
1 pt	1 pt	1 pt	1 pt
1.5 pt	1.5 pt	1.5 pt	1.5 pt
2 pt	2 pt	2 pt	2 pt
2.5 pt	2.5 pt	2.5 pt	2.5 pt
3 pt	3 pt	3 pt	3 pt
4 pt	4 pt	4 pt	4 pt
5 pt	5 pt	5 pt	5 pt
6 pt	6 pt	6 pt	6 pt
7 pt	7 pt	7 pt	7 pt
8 pt	8 pt	8 pt	8 pt
9 pt	9 pt	9 pt	9 pt
10 pt	10 pt	10 pt	10 pt

THICK-THICK

0.25 pt

0.5 pt

0.75 pt

1 pt

1.5 pt

2 pt

2.5 pt

3 pt

4 pt

5 pt

6 pt

7 pt

8 pt

9 pt

10 pt

Black: 75% Tint HEX #636466	Black: 50% Tint HEX #939598	Black: 25% Tint HEX #C7C8CA	Black: 10% Tint HEX #E6E7E8
0.25 pt	0.25 pt	0.25 pt	0.25 pt
0.5 pt	0.5 pt	0.5 pt	0.5 pt
0.75 pt	0.75 pt	0.75 pt	0.75 pt
1 pt	1 pt	1 pt	1 pt
1.5 pt	1.5 pt	1.5 pt	1.5 pt
2 pt	2 pt	2 pt	2 pt
2.5 pt	2.5 pt	2.5 pt	2.5 pt
3 pt	3 pt	3 pt	3 pt
4 pt	4 pt	4 pt	4 pt
5 pt	5 pt	5 pt	5 pt
6 pt	6 pt	6 pt	6 pt
7 pt	7 pt	7 pt	7 pt
8 pt	8 pt	8 pt	8 pt
9 pt	9 pt	9 pt	9 pt
10 pt	10 pt	10 pt	10 pt

THIN-THICK

0.25 pt

0.5 pt

0.75 pt

1 pt

1.5 pt

2 pt

2.5 pt

3 pt

4 pt

5 pt

6 pt

7 pt

8 pt

9 pt

10 pt

Black: 75% Tint HEX #636466	Black: 50% Tint HEX #939598	Black: 25% Tint HEX #C7C8CA	Black: 10% Tint HEX #E6E7E8
0.25 pt	0.25 pt	0.25 pt	0.25 pt
0.5 pt	0.5 pt	0.5 pt	0.5 pt
0.75 pt	0.75 pt	0.75 pt	0.75 pt
1 pt	1 pt	1 pt	1 pt
1.5 pt	1.5 pt	1.5 pt	1.5 pt
2 pt	2 pt	2 pt	2 pt
2.5 pt	2.5 pt	2.5 pt	2.5 pt
3 pt	3 pt	3 pt	3 pt
4 pt	4 pt	4 pt	4 pt
5 pt	5 pt	5 pt	5 pt
6 pt	6 pt	6 pt	6 pt
7 pt	7 pt	7 pt	7 pt
8 pt	8 pt	8 pt	8 pt
9 pt	9 pt	9 pt	9 pt
10 pt	10 pt	10 pt	10 pt

THICK-THIN

0.25 pt

0.5 pt

0.75 pt

1 pt

1.5 pt

2 pt

2.5 pt

3 pt

4 pt

5 pt

6 pt

7 pt

8 pt

9 pt

10 pt

Black: 75% Tint HEX #636466	Black: 50% Tint HEX #939598	Black: 25% Tint HEX #C7C8CA	Black: 10% Tint HEX #E6E7E8
0.25 pt	0.25 pt	0.25 pt	0.25 pt
0.5 pt	0.5 pt	0.5 pt	0.5 pt
0.75 pt	0.75 pt	0.75 pt	0.75 pt
1 pt	1 pt	1 pt	1 pt
1.5 pt	1.5 pt	1.5 pt	1.5 pt
2 pt	2 pt	2 pt	2 pt
2.5 pt	2.5 pt	2.5 pt	2.5 pt
3 pt	3 pt	3 pt	3 pt
4 pt	4 pt	4 pt	4 pt
5 pt	5 pt	5 pt	5 pt
6 pt	6 pt	6 pt	6 pt
7 pt	7 pt	7 pt	7 pt
8 pt	8 pt	8 pt	8 pt
9 pt	9 pt	9 pt	9 pt
10 pt	10 pt	10 pt	10 pt

TRIPLE

0.25 pt

0.5 pt

0.75 pt

1 pt

1.5 pt

2 pt

2.5 pt

3 pt

4 pt

5 pt

6 pt

7 pt

8 pt

9 pt

10 pt

Black: 75% Tint HEX #636466	Black: 50% Tint HEX #939598	Black: 25% Tint HEX #C7C8CA	Black: 10% Tint HEX #E6E7E8
0.25 pt	0.25 pt	0.25 pt	0.25 pt
0.5 pt	0.5 pt	0.5 pt	0.5 pt
0.75 pt	0.75 pt	0.75 pt	0.75 pt
1 pt	1 pt	1 pt	1 pt
1.5 pt	1.5 pt	1.5 pt	1.5 pt
2 pt	2 pt	2 pt	2 pt
2.5 pt	2.5 pt	2.5 pt	2.5 pt
3 pt	3 pt	3 pt	3 pt
4 pt	4 pt	4 pt	4 pt
5 pt	5 pt	5 pt	5 pt
6 pt	6 pt	6 pt	6 pt
7 pt	7 pt	7 pt	7 pt
8 pt	8 pt	8 pt	8 pt
9 pt	9 pt	9 pt	9 pt
10 pt	10 pt	10 pt	10 pt

THICK-THIN-THICK

0.25 pt

0.5 pt

0.75 pt

1 pt

1.5 pt

2 pt

2.5 pt

3 pt

4 pt

5 pt

6 pt

7 pt

8 pt

9 pt

10 pt

Black: 75% Tint HEX #636466	Black: 50% Tint HEX #939598	Black: 25% Tint HEX #C7C8CA	Black: 10% Tint HEX #E6E7E8
0.25 pt	0.25 pt	0.25 pt	0.25 pt
0.5 pt	0.5 pt	0.5 pt	0.5 pt
0.75 pt	0.75 pt	0.75 pt	0.75 pt
1 pt	1 pt	1 pt	1 pt
1.5 pt	1.5 pt	1.5 pt	1.5 pt
2 pt	2 pt	2 pt	2 pt
2.5 pt	2.5 pt	2.5 pt	2.5 pt
3 pt	3 pt	3 pt	3 pt
4 pt	4 pt	4 pt	4 pt
5 pt	5 pt	5 pt	5 pt
6 pt	6 pt	6 pt	6 pt
7 pt	7 pt	7 pt	7 pt
8 pt	8 pt	8 pt	8 pt
9 pt	9 pt	9 pt	9 pt
10 pt	10 pt	10 pt	10 pt

THIN-THICK-THIN

0.25 pt

0.5 pt

0.75 pt

1 pt

1.5 pt

2 pt

2.5 pt

3 pt

4 pt

5 pt

6 pt

7 pt

8 pt

9 pt

10 pt

Black: 75% Tint HEX #636466	Black: 50% Tint HEX #939598	Black: 25% Tint HEX #C7C8CA	Black: 10% Tint HEX #E6E7E8
0.25 pt	0.25 pt	0.25 pt	0.25 pt
0.5 pt	0.5 pt	0.5 pt	0.5 pt
0.75 pt	0.75 pt	0.75 pt	0.75 pt
1 pt	1 pt	1 pt	1 pt
1.5 pt	1.5 pt	1.5 pt	1.5 pt
2 pt	2 pt	2 pt	2 pt
2.5 pt	2.5 pt	2.5 pt	2.5 pt
3 pt	3 pt	3 pt	3 pt
4 pt	4 pt	4 pt	4 pt
5 pt	5 pt	5 pt	5 pt
6 pt	6 pt	6 pt	6 pt
7 pt	7 pt	7 pt	7 pt
8 pt	8 pt	8 pt	8 pt
9 pt	9 pt	9 pt	9 pt
10 pt	10 pt	10 pt	10 pt

WHITE DIAMONDS

0.25 pt

0.5 pt

0.75 pt

1 pt

1.5 pt

2 pt

2.5 pt

3 pt

4 pt

5 pt

6 pt

7 pt

8 pt

9 pt

10 pt

Black: 75% Tint HEX #636466	Black: 50% Tint HEX #939598	Black: 25% Tint HEX #C7C8CA	Black: 10% Tint HEX #E6E7E8
0.25 pt	0.25 pt	0.25 pt	0.25 pt
0.5 pt	0.5 pt	0.5 pt	0.5 pt
0.75 pt	0.75 pt	0.75 pt	0.75 pt
1 pt	1 pt	1 pt	1 pt
1.5 pt	1.5 pt	1.5 pt	1.5 pt
2 pt	2 pt	2 pt	2 pt
2.5 pt	2.5 pt	2.5 pt	2.5 pt
3 pt	3 pt	3 pt	3 pt
4 pt	4 pt	4 pt	4 pt
5 pt	5 pt	5 pt	5 pt
6 pt	6 pt	6 pt	6 pt
7 pt	7 pt	7 pt	7 pt
8 pt	8 pt	8 pt	8 pt
9 pt	9 pt	9 pt	9 pt
10 pt	10 pt	10 pt	10 pt

JAPANESE DOTS

0.25 pt

0.5 pt

0.75 pt

1 pt

1.5 pt

2 pt

2.5 pt

3 pt

4 pt

5 pt

6 pt

7 pt

8 pt

9 pt

10 pt

Black: 75% Tint	**Black: 50% Tint**	**Black: 25% Tint**	**Black: 10% Tint**
HEX #636466	HEX #939598	HEX #C7C8CA	HEX #E6E7E8
0.25 pt	0.25 pt	0.25 pt	0.25 pt
0.5 pt	0.5 pt	0.5 pt	0.5 pt
0.75 pt	0.75 pt	0.75 pt	0.75 pt
1 pt	1 pt	1 pt	1 pt
1.5 pt	1.5 pt	1.5 pt	1.5 pt
2 pt	2 pt	2 pt	2 pt
2.5 pt	2.5 pt	2.5 pt	2.5 pt
3 pt	3 pt	3 pt	3 pt
4 pt	4 pt	4 pt	4 pt
5 pt	5 pt	5 pt	5 pt
6 pt	6 pt	6 pt	6 pt
7 pt	7 pt	7 pt	7 pt
8 pt	8 pt	8 pt	8 pt
9 pt	9 pt	9 pt	9 pt
10 pt	10 pt	10 pt	10 pt

DOTTED

0.25 pt

0.5 pt

0.75 pt

1 pt

1.5 pt

2 pt

2.5 pt

3 pt

4 pt

5 pt

6 pt

7 pt

8 pt

9 pt

10 pt

Black: 75% Tint HEX #636466	Black: 50% Tint HEX #939598	Black: 25% Tint HEX #C7C8CA	Black: 10% Tint HEX #E6E7E8
0.25 pt	0.25 pt	0.25 pt	0.25 pt
0.5 pt	0.5 pt	0.5 pt	0.5 pt
0.75 pt	0.75 pt	0.75 pt	0.75 pt
1 pt	1 pt	1 pt	1 pt
1.5 pt	1.5 pt	1.5 pt	1.5 pt
2 pt	2 pt	2 pt	2 pt
2.5 pt	2.5 pt	2.5 pt	2.5 pt
3 pt	3 pt	3 pt	3 pt
4 pt	4 pt	4 pt	4 pt
5 pt	5 pt	5 pt	5 pt
6 pt	6 pt	6 pt	6 pt
7 pt	7 pt	7 pt	7 pt
8 pt	8 pt	8 pt	8 pt
9 pt	9 pt	9 pt	9 pt
10 pt	10 pt	10 pt	10 pt

DASHED

0.25 pt

0.5 pt

0.75 pt

1 pt

1.5 pt

2 pt

2.5 pt

3 pt

4 pt

5 pt

6 pt

7 pt

8 pt

9 pt

10 pt

Black: 75% Tint	Black: 50% Tint	Black: 25% Tint	Black: 10% Tint
HEX #636466	HEX #939598	HEX #C7C8CA	HEX #E6E7E8
0.25 pt	0.25 pt	0.25 pt	0.25 pt
0.5 pt	0.5 pt	0.5 pt	0.5 pt
0.75 pt	0.75 pt	0.75 pt	0.75 pt
1 pt	1 pt	1 pt	1 pt
1.5 pt	1.5 pt	1.5 pt	1.5 pt
2 pt	2 pt	2 pt	2 pt
2.5 pt	2.5 pt	2.5 pt	2.5 pt
3 pt	3 pt	3 pt	3 pt
4 pt	4 pt	4 pt	4 pt
5 pt	5 pt	5 pt	5 pt
6 pt	6 pt	6 pt	6 pt
7 pt	7 pt	7 pt	7 pt
8 pt	8 pt	8 pt	8 pt
9 pt	9 pt	9 pt	9 pt
10 pt	10 pt	10 pt	10 pt

DASHED (3 & 2)

0.25 pt

0.5 pt

0.75 pt

1 pt

1.5 pt

2 pt

2.5 pt

3 pt

4 pt

5 pt

6 pt

7 pt

8 pt

9 pt

10 pt

Black: 75% Tint	Black: 50% Tint	Black: 25% Tint	Black: 10% Tint
HEX #636466	HEX #939598	HEX #C7C8CA	HEX #E6E7E8
0.25 pt	0.25 pt	0.25 pt	0.25 pt
0.5 pt	0.5 pt	0.5 pt	0.5 pt
0.75 pt	0.75 pt	0.75 pt	0.75 pt
1 pt	1 pt	1 pt	1 pt
1.5 pt	1.5 pt	1.5 pt	1.5 pt
2 pt	2 pt	2 pt	2 pt
2.5 pt	2.5 pt	2.5 pt	2.5 pt
3 pt	3 pt	3 pt	3 pt
4 pt	4 pt	4 pt	4 pt
5 pt	5 pt	5 pt	5 pt
6 pt	6 pt	6 pt	6 pt
7 pt	7 pt	7 pt	7 pt
8 pt	8 pt	8 pt	8 pt
9 pt	9 pt	9 pt	9 pt
10 pt	10 pt	10 pt	10 pt

DASHED (4 & 4)

0.25 pt

0.5 pt

0.75 pt

1 pt

1.5 pt

2 pt

2.5 pt

3 pt

4 pt

5 pt

6 pt

7 pt

8 pt

9 pt

10 pt

| Black: 75% Tint | Black: 50% Tint | Black: 25% Tint | Black: 10% Tint |
HEX #636466	HEX #939598	HEX #C7C8CA	HEX #E6E7E8
0.25 pt	0.25 pt	0.25 pt	0.25 pt
0.5 pt	0.5 pt	0.5 pt	0.5 pt
0.75 pt	0.75 pt	0.75 pt	0.75 pt
1 pt	1 pt	1 pt	1 pt
1.5 pt	1.5 pt	1.5 pt	1.5 pt
2 pt	2 pt	2 pt	2 pt
2.5 pt	2.5 pt	2.5 pt	2.5 pt
3 pt	3 pt	3 pt	3 pt
4 pt	4 pt	4 pt	4 pt
5 pt	5 pt	5 pt	5 pt
6 pt	6 pt	6 pt	6 pt
7 pt	7 pt	7 pt	7 pt
8 pt	8 pt	8 pt	8 pt
9 pt	9 pt	9 pt	9 pt
10 pt	10 pt	10 pt	10 pt

STRAIGHT HASH

0.25 pt

0.5 pt

0.75 pt

1 pt

1.5 pt

2 pt

2.5 pt

3 pt

4 pt

5 pt

6 pt

7 pt

8 pt

9 pt

10 pt

Black: 75% Tint HEX #636466	Black: 50% Tint HEX #939598	Black: 25% Tint HEX #C7C8CA	Black: 10% Tint HEX #E6E7E8
0.25 pt	0.25 pt	0.25 pt	0.25 pt
0.5 pt	0.5 pt	0.5 pt	0.5 pt
0.75 pt	0.75 pt	0.75 pt	0.75 pt
1 pt	1 pt	1 pt	1 pt
1.5 pt	1.5 pt	1.5 pt	1.5 pt
2 pt	2 pt	2 pt	2 pt
2.5 pt	2.5 pt	2.5 pt	2.5 pt
3 pt	3 pt	3 pt	3 pt
4 pt	4 pt	4 pt	4 pt
5 pt	5 pt	5 pt	5 pt
6 pt	6 pt	6 pt	6 pt
7 pt	7 pt	7 pt	7 pt
8 pt	8 pt	8 pt	8 pt
9 pt	9 pt	9 pt	9 pt
10 pt	10 pt	10 pt	10 pt

LEFT SLANT HASH

0.25 pt

0.5 pt

0.75 pt

1 pt

1.5 pt

2 pt

2.5 pt

3 pt

4 pt

5 pt

6 pt

7 pt

8 pt

9 pt

10 pt

Black: 75% Tint **HEX #636466**	**Black: 50% Tint** **HEX #939598**	**Black: 25% Tint** **HEX #C7C8CA**	**Black: 10% Tint** **HEX #E6E7E8**
0.25 pt	0.25 pt	0.25 pt	0.25 pt
0.5 pt	0.5 pt	0.5 pt	0.5 pt
0.75 pt	0.75 pt	0.75 pt	0.75 pt
1 pt	1 pt	1 pt	1 pt
1.5 pt	1.5 pt	1.5 pt	1.5 pt
2 pt	2 pt	2 pt	2 pt
2.5 pt	2.5 pt	2.5 pt	2.5 pt
3 pt	3 pt	3 pt	3 pt
4 pt	4 pt	4 pt	4 pt
5 pt	5 pt	5 pt	5 pt
6 pt	6 pt	6 pt	6 pt
7 pt	7 pt	7 pt	7 pt
8 pt	8 pt	8 pt	8 pt
9 pt	9 pt	9 pt	9 pt
10 pt	10 pt	10 pt	10 pt

RIGHT SLANT HASH

0.25 pt

0.5 pt

0.75 pt

1 pt

1.5 pt

2 pt

2.5 pt

3 pt

4 pt

5 pt

6 pt

7 pt

8 pt

9 pt

10 pt

Black: 75% Tint HEX #636466	Black: 50% Tint HEX #939598	Black: 25% Tint HEX #C7C8CA	Black: 10% Tint HEX #E6E7E8
0.25 pt	0.25 pt	0.25 pt	0.25 pt
0.5 pt	0.5 pt	0.5 pt	0.5 pt
0.75 pt	0.75 pt	0.75 pt	0.75 pt
1 pt	1 pt	1 pt	1 pt
1.5 pt	1.5 pt	1.5 pt	1.5 pt
2 pt	2 pt	2 pt	2 pt
2.5 pt	2.5 pt	2.5 pt	2.5 pt
3 pt	3 pt	3 pt	3 pt
4 pt	4 pt	4 pt	4 pt
5 pt	5 pt	5 pt	5 pt
6 pt	6 pt	6 pt	6 pt
7 pt	7 pt	7 pt	7 pt
8 pt	8 pt	8 pt	8 pt
9 pt	9 pt	9 pt	9 pt
10 pt	10 pt	10 pt	10 pt

WAVY

0.25 pt

0.5 pt

0.75 pt

1 pt

1.5 pt

2 pt

2.5 pt

3 pt

4 pt

5 pt

6 pt

7 pt

8 pt

9 pt

10 pt

Black: 75% Tint HEX #636466	Black: 50% Tint HEX #939598	Black: 25% Tint HEX #C7C8CA	Black: 10% Tint HEX #E6E7E8
0.25 pt	0.25 pt	0.25 pt	0.25 pt
0.5 pt	0.5 pt	0.5 pt	0.5 pt
0.75 pt	0.75 pt	0.75 pt	0.75 pt
1 pt	1 pt	1 pt	1 pt
1.5 pt	1.5 pt	1.5 pt	1.5 pt
2 pt	2 pt	2 pt	2 pt
2.5 pt	2.5 pt	2.5 pt	2.5 pt
3 pt	3 pt	3 pt	3 pt
4 pt	4 pt	4 pt	4 pt
5 pt	5 pt	5 pt	5 pt
6 pt	6 pt	6 pt	6 pt
7 pt	7 pt	7 pt	7 pt
8 pt	8 pt	8 pt	8 pt
9 pt	9 pt	9 pt	9 pt
10 pt	10 pt	10 pt	10 pt

NOTES:

FONTS

ADOBE GARAMOND PRO

4 pt
The quick brown fox jumps over the lazy dog. 0 1 2 3 4 5 6 7 8 9. *The quick brown fox jumps over the lazy dog. 0 1 2 3 4 5 6 7 8 9.* **The quick brown fox jumps over the lazy dog. 0 1 2 3 4 5 6 7 8 9.**

5 pt
The quick brown fox jumps over the lazy dog. 0 1 2 3 4 5 6 7 8 9. *The quick brown fox jumps over the lazy dog. 0 1 2 3 4 5 6 7 8 9.* **The quick brown fox jumps over the lazy dog. 0 1 2 3 4 5 6 7 8 9.**

6 pt
The quick brown fox jumps over the lazy dog. 0 1 2 3 4 5 6 7 8 9. *The quick brown fox jumps over the lazy dog. 0 1 2 3 4 5 6 7 8 9.* **The quick brown fox jumps over the lazy dog. 0 1 2 3 4 5 6 7 8 9.**

7 pt
The quick brown fox jumps over the lazy dog. 0 1 2 3 4 5 6 7 8 9. *The quick brown fox jumps over the lazy dog. 0 1 2 3 4 5 6 7 8 9.* **The quick brown fox jumps over the lazy dog. 0 1 2 3 4 5 6 7 8 9.**

8 pt
The quick brown fox jumps over the lazy dog. 0 1 2 3 4 5 6 7 8 9. *The quick brown fox jumps over the lazy dog. 0 1 2 3 4 5 6 7 8 9.* **The quick brown fox jumps over the lazy dog. 0 1 2 3 4 5 6 7 8 9.**

9 pt
The quick brown fox jumps over the lazy dog. 0 1 2 3 4 5 6 7 8 9. *The quick brown fox jumps over the lazy dog. 0 1 2 3 4 5 6 7 8 9.* **The quick brown fox jumps over the lazy dog. 0 1 2 3 4 5 6 7 8 9.**

10 pt
The quick brown fox jumps over the lazy dog. 0 1 2 3 4 5 6 7 8 9. *The quick brown fox jumps over the lazy dog. 0 1 2 3 4 5 6 7 8 9.* **The quick brown fox jumps over the lazy dog. 0 1 2 3 4 5 6 7 8 9.**

12 pt
The quick brown fox jumps over the lazy dog. 0 1 2 3 4 5 6 7 8 9. *The quick brown fox jumps over the lazy dog. 0 1 2 3 4 5 6 7 8 9.* **The quick brown fox jumps over the lazy dog. 0 1 2 3 4 5 6 7 8 9.**

14 pt
The quick brown fox jumps over the lazy dog. 0 1 2 3 4 5 6 7 8 9. *The quick brown fox jumps over the lazy dog. 0 1 2 3 4 5 6 7 8 9.* **The quick brown fox jumps over the lazy dog. 0 1 2 3 4 5 6 7 8 9.**

16 pt
The quick brown fox jumps over the lazy dog. 0 1 2 3 4 5 6 7 8 9. *The quick brown fox jumps over the lazy dog. 0 1 2 3 4 5 6 7 8 9.* **The quick brown fox jumps over the lazy dog. 0 1 2 3 4 5 6 7 8 9.**

18 pt
The quick brown fox jumps over the lazy dog. 0 1 2

3 4 5 6 7 8 9. *The quick brown fox jumps over the lazy dog. 0 1 2 3 4 5 6 7 8 9.* **The quick brown fox jumps over the lazy dog. 0 1 2 3 4 5 6 7 8 9.**

24 pt

The quick brown fox jumps over the lazy dog. 0 1 2 3 4 5 6 7 8 9. *The quick brown fox jumps over the lazy dog. 0 1 2 3 4 5 6 7 8 9.* **The quick brown fox jumps over the lazy dog. 0 1 2 3 4 5 6 7 8 9.**

36 pt

The quick brown fox jumps over the lazy dog. 0 1 2 3 4 5 6 7 8 9. *The quick brown fox jumps over the lazy dog. 0 1 2 3 4 5 6 7 8 9.* **The quick brown fox jumps over the lazy dog. 0 1 2 3 4 5 6 7 8 9.**

Black: 75% Tint
HEX #636466

6 pt
The quick brown fox jumps over the lazy dog. 0 1 2 3 4 5 6 7 8 9. *The quick brown fox jumps over the lazy dog. 0 1 2 3 4 5 6 7 8 9.* **The quick brown fox jumps over the lazy dog. 0 1 2 3 4 5 6 7 8 9.**

7 pt
The quick brown fox jumps over the lazy dog. 0 1 2 3 4 5 6 7 8 9. *The quick brown fox jumps over the lazy dog. 0 1 2 3 4 5 6 7 8 9.* **The quick brown fox jumps over the lazy dog. 0 1 2 3 4 5 6 7 8 9.**

8 pt
The quick brown fox jumps over the lazy dog. 0 1 2 3 4 5 6 7 8 9. *The quick brown fox jumps over the lazy dog. 0 1 2 3 4 5 6 7 8 9.* **The quick brown fox jumps over the lazy dog. 0 1 2 3 4 5 6 7 8 9.**

9 pt
The quick brown fox jumps over the lazy dog. 0 1 2 3 4 5 6 7 8 9. *The quick brown fox jumps over the lazy dog. 0 1 2 3 4 5 6 7 8 9.* **The quick brown fox jumps over the lazy dog. 0 1 2 3 4 5 6 7 8 9.**

10 pt
The quick brown fox jumps over the lazy dog. 0 1 2 3 4 5 6 7 8 9. *The quick brown fox jumps over the lazy dog. 0 1 2 3 4 5 6 7 8 9.* **The quick brown fox jumps over the lazy dog. 0 1 2 3 4 5 6 7 8 9.**

12 pt
The quick brown fox jumps over the lazy dog. 0 1 2 3 4 5 6 7 8 9. *The quick brown fox jumps over the lazy dog. 0 1 2 3 4 5 6 7 8 9.* **The quick brown fox jumps over the lazy dog. 0 1 2 3 4 5 6 7 8 9.**

14 pt
The quick brown fox jumps over the lazy dog. 0 1 2 3 4 5 6 7 8 9. *The quick brown fox jumps over the lazy dog. 0 1 2 3 4 5 6 7 8 9.* **The quick brown fox jumps over the lazy dog. 0 1 2 3 4 5 6 7 8 9.**

Black: 50% Tint
HEX #939598

6 pt
The quick brown fox jumps over the lazy dog. 0 1 2 3 4 5 6 7 8 9. *The quick brown fox jumps over the lazy dog. 0 1 2 3 4 5 6 7 8 9.* **The quick brown fox jumps over the lazy dog. 0 1 2 3 4 5 6 7 8 9.**

7 pt
The quick brown fox jumps over the lazy dog. 0 1 2 3 4 5 6 7 8 9. *The quick brown fox jumps over the lazy dog. 0 1 2 3 4 5 6 7 8 9.* **The quick brown fox jumps over the lazy dog. 0 1 2 3 4 5 6 7 8 9.**

8 pt
The quick brown fox jumps over the lazy dog. 0 1 2 3 4 5 6 7 8 9. *The quick brown fox jumps over the lazy dog. 0 1 2 3 4 5 6 7 8 9.* **The quick brown fox jumps over the lazy dog. 0 1 2 3 4 5 6 7 8 9.**

9 pt
The quick brown fox jumps over the lazy dog. 0 1 2 3 4 5 6 7 8 9. *The quick brown fox jumps over the lazy dog. 0 1 2 3 4 5 6 7 8 9.* **The quick brown fox jumps over the lazy dog. 0 1 2 3 4 5 6 7 8 9.**

10 pt
The quick brown fox jumps over the lazy dog. 0 1 2 3 4 5 6 7 8 9. *The quick brown fox jumps over the lazy dog. 0 1 2 3 4 5 6 7 8 9.* **The quick brown fox jumps over the lazy dog. 0 1 2 3 4 5 6 7 8 9.**

12 pt
The quick brown fox jumps over the lazy dog. 0 1 2 3 4 5 6 7 8 9. *The quick brown fox jumps over the lazy dog. 0 1 2 3 4 5 6 7 8 9.* **The quick brown fox jumps over the lazy dog. 0 1 2 3 4 5 6 7 8 9.**

14 pt
The quick brown fox jumps over the lazy dog. 0 1 2 3 4 5 6 7 8 9. *The quick brown fox jumps over the lazy dog. 0 1 2 3 4 5 6 7 8 9.* **The quick brown fox jumps over the lazy dog. 0 1 2 3 4 5 6 7 8 9.**

Black: 25% Tint
HEX #C7C8CA

6 pt

The quick brown fox jumps over the lazy dog. 0 1 2 3 4 5 6 7 8 9. *The quick brown fox jumps over the lazy dog. 0 1 2 3 4 5 6 7 8 9.* **The quick brown fox jumps over the lazy dog. 0 1 2 3 4 5 6 7 8 9.**

7 pt

The quick brown fox jumps over the lazy dog. 0 1 2 3 4 5 6 7 8 9. *The quick brown fox jumps over the lazy dog. 0 1 2 3 4 5 6 7 8 9.* **The quick brown fox jumps over the lazy dog. 0 1 2 3 4 5 6 7 8 9.**

8 pt

The quick brown fox jumps over the lazy dog. 0 1 2 3 4 5 6 7 8 9. *The quick brown fox jumps over the lazy dog. 0 1 2 3 4 5 6 7 8 9.* **The quick brown fox jumps over the lazy dog. 0 1 2 3 4 5 6 7 8 9.**

9 pt

The quick brown fox jumps over the lazy dog. 0 1 2 3 4 5 6 7 8 9. *The quick brown fox jumps over the lazy dog. 0 1 2 3 4 5 6 7 8 9.* **The quick brown fox jumps over the lazy dog. 0 1 2 3 4 5 6 7 8 9.**

10 pt

The quick brown fox jumps over the lazy dog. 0 1 2 3 4 5 6 7 8 9. *The quick brown fox jumps over the lazy dog. 0 1 2 3 4 5 6 7 8 9.* **The quick brown fox jumps over the lazy dog. 0 1 2 3 4 5 6 7 8 9.**

12 pt

The quick brown fox jumps over the lazy dog. 0 1 2 3 4 5 6 7 8 9. *The quick brown fox jumps over the lazy dog. 0 1 2 3 4 5 6 7 8 9.* **The quick brown fox jumps over the lazy dog. 0 1 2 3 4 5 6 7 8 9.**

14 pt

The quick brown fox jumps over the lazy dog. 0 1 2 3 4 5 6 7 8 9. *The quick brown fox jumps over the lazy dog. 0 1 2 3 4 5 6 7 8 9.* **The quick brown fox jumps over the lazy dog. 0 1 2 3 4 5 6 7 8 9.**

Black: 10% Tint
HEX #E6E7E8

6 pt

The quick brown fox jumps over the lazy dog. 0 1 2 3 4 5 6 7 8 9. *The quick brown fox jumps over the lazy dog. 0 1 2 3 4 5 6 7 8 9.* **The quick brown fox jumps over the lazy dog. 0 1 2 3 4 5 6 7 8 9.**

7 pt

The quick brown fox jumps over the lazy dog. 0 1 2 3 4 5 6 7 8 9. *The quick brown fox jumps over the lazy dog. 0 1 2 3 4 5 6 7 8 9.* **The quick brown fox jumps over the lazy dog. 0 1 2 3 4 5 6 7 8 9.**

8 pt

The quick brown fox jumps over the lazy dog. 0 1 2 3 4 5 6 7 8 9. *The quick brown fox jumps over the lazy dog. 0 1 2 3 4 5 6 7 8 9.* **The quick brown fox jumps over the lazy dog. 0 1 2 3 4 5 6 7 8 9.**

9 pt

The quick brown fox jumps over the lazy dog. 0 1 2 3 4 5 6 7 8 9. *The quick brown fox jumps over the lazy dog. 0 1 2 3 4 5 6 7 8 9.* **The quick brown fox jumps over the lazy dog. 0 1 2 3 4 5 6 7 8 9.**

10 pt

The quick brown fox jumps over the lazy dog. 0 1 2 3 4 5 6 7 8 9. *The quick brown fox jumps over the lazy dog. 0 1 2 3 4 5 6 7 8 9.* **The quick brown fox jumps over the lazy dog. 0 1 2 3 4 5 6 7 8 9.**

12 pt

The quick brown fox jumps over the lazy dog. 0 1 2 3 4 5 6 7 8 9. *The quick brown fox jumps over the lazy dog. 0 1 2 3 4 5 6 7 8 9.* **The quick brown fox jumps over the lazy dog. 0 1 2 3 4 5 6 7 8 9.**

14 pt

The quick brown fox jumps over the lazy dog. 0 1 2 3 4 5 6 7 8 9. *The quick brown fox jumps over the lazy dog. 0 1 2 3 4 5 6 7 8 9.* **The quick brown fox jumps over the lazy dog. 0 1 2 3 4 5 6 7 8 9.**

BASKERVILLE

4 pt

The quick brown fox jumps over the lazy dog. 0 1 2 3 4 5 6 7 8 9. *The quick brown fox jumps over the lazy dog. 0 1 2 3 4 5 6 7 8 9.* **The quick brown fox jumps over the lazy dog. 0 1 2 3 4 5 6 7 8 9.**

5 pt

The quick brown fox jumps over the lazy dog. 0 1 2 3 4 5 6 7 8 9. *The quick brown fox jumps over the lazy dog. 0 1 2 3 4 5 6 7 8 9.* **The quick brown fox jumps over the lazy dog. 0 1 2 3 4 5 6 7 8 9.**

6 pt

The quick brown fox jumps over the lazy dog. 0 1 2 3 4 5 6 7 8 9. *The quick brown fox jumps over the lazy dog. 0 1 2 3 4 5 6 7 8 9.* **The quick brown fox jumps over the lazy dog. 0 1 2 3 4 5 6 7 8 9.**

7 pt

The quick brown fox jumps over the lazy dog. 0 1 2 3 4 5 6 7 8 9. *The quick brown fox jumps over the lazy dog. 0 1 2 3 4 5 6 7 8 9.* **The quick brown fox jumps over the lazy dog. 0 1 2 3 4 5 6 7 8 9.**

8 pt

The quick brown fox jumps over the lazy dog. 0 1 2 3 4 5 6 7 8 9. *The quick brown fox jumps over the lazy dog. 0 1 2 3 4 5 6 7 8 9.* **The quick brown fox jumps over the lazy dog. 0 1 2 3 4 5 6 7 8 9.**

9 pt

The quick brown fox jumps over the lazy dog. 0 1 2 3 4 5 6 7 8 9. *The quick brown fox jumps over the lazy dog. 0 1 2 3 4 5 6 7 8 9.* **The quick brown fox jumps over the lazy dog. 0 1 2 3 4 5 6 7 8 9.**

10 pt

The quick brown fox jumps over the lazy dog. 0 1 2 3 4 5 6 7 8 9. *The quick brown fox jumps over the lazy dog. 0 1 2 3 4 5 6 7 8 9.* **The quick brown fox jumps over the lazy dog. 0 1 2 3 4 5 6 7 8 9.**

12 pt

The quick brown fox jumps over the lazy dog. 0 1 2 3 4 5 6 7 8 9. *The quick brown fox jumps over the lazy dog. 0 1 2 3 4 5 6 7 8 9.* **The quick brown fox jumps over the lazy dog. 0 1 2 3 4 5 6 7 8 9.**

14 pt

The quick brown fox jumps over the lazy dog. 0 1 2 3 4 5 6 7 8 9. *The quick brown fox jumps over the lazy dog. 0 1 2 3 4 5 6 7 8 9.* **The quick brown fox jumps over the lazy dog. 0 1 2 3 4 5 6 7 8 9.**

16 pt

The quick brown fox jumps over the lazy dog. 0 1 2 3 4 5 6 7 8 9. *The quick brown fox jumps over the lazy dog. 0 1 2 3 4 5 6 7 8 9.* **The quick brown fox jumps over the lazy dog. 0 1 2 3 4 5 6 7 8 9.**

18 pt

The quick brown fox jumps over the lazy dog. 0 1 2 3 4 5 6 7 8 9. *The quick brown fox jumps over the lazy dog. 0 1 2 3 4 5 6 7 8 9.* **The quick brown fox jumps over the lazy dog. 0 1 2 3 4 5 6 7 8 9.**

24 pt

The quick brown fox jumps over the lazy dog. 0 1 2 3 4 5 6 7 8 9. *The quick brown fox jumps over the lazy dog. 0 1 2 3 4 5 6 7 8 9.* **The quick brown fox jumps over the lazy dog. 0 1 2 3 4 5 6 7 8 9.**

36 pt

The quick brown fox jumps over the lazy dog. 0 1 2 3 4 5 6 7 8 9. *The quick brown fox jumps over the lazy dog. 0 1 2 3 4 5 6 7 8 9.* **The quick brown fox jumps over the lazy dog. 0 1 2 3 4 5 6 7 8 9.**

Black: 75% Tint
HEX #636466

6 pt
The quick brown fox jumps over the lazy dog. 0 1 2 3 4 5 6 7 8 9. *The quick brown fox jumps over the lazy dog. 0 1 2 3 4 5 6 7 8 9.* **The quick brown fox jumps over the lazy dog. 0 1 2 3 4 5 6 7 8 9.**

7 pt
The quick brown fox jumps over the lazy dog. 0 1 2 3 4 5 6 7 8 9. *The quick brown fox jumps over the lazy dog. 0 1 2 3 4 5 6 7 8 9.* **The quick brown fox jumps over the lazy dog. 0 1 2 3 4 5 6 7 8 9.**

8 pt
The quick brown fox jumps over the lazy dog. 0 1 2 3 4 5 6 7 8 9. *The quick brown fox jumps over the lazy dog. 0 1 2 3 4 5 6 7 8 9.* **The quick brown fox jumps over the lazy dog. 0 1 2 3 4 5 6 7 8 9.**

9 pt
The quick brown fox jumps over the lazy dog. 0 1 2 3 4 5 6 7 8 9. *The quick brown fox jumps over the lazy dog. 0 1 2 3 4 5 6 7 8 9.* **The quick brown fox jumps over the lazy dog. 0 1 2 3 4 5 6 7 8 9.**

10 pt
The quick brown fox jumps over the lazy dog. 0 1 2 3 4 5 6 7 8 9. *The quick brown fox jumps over the lazy dog. 0 1 2 3 4 5 6 7 8 9.* **The quick brown fox jumps over the lazy dog. 0 1 2 3 4 5 6 7 8 9.**

12 pt
The quick brown fox jumps over the lazy dog. 0 1 2 3 4 5 6 7 8 9. *The quick brown fox jumps over the lazy dog. 0 1 2 3 4 5 6 7 8 9.* **The quick brown fox jumps over the lazy dog. 0 1 2 3 4 5 6 7 8 9.**

14 pt
The quick brown fox jumps over the lazy dog. 0 1 2 3 4 5 6 7 8 9. *The quick brown fox jumps over the lazy dog. 0 1 2 3 4 5 6 7 8 9.* **The quick brown fox jumps over the lazy dog. 0 1 2 3 4 5 6 7 8 9.**

Black: 50% Tint
HEX #939598

6 pt
The quick brown fox jumps over the lazy dog. 0 1 2 3 4 5 6 7 8 9. *The quick brown fox jumps over the lazy dog. 0 1 2 3 4 5 6 7 8 9.* **The quick brown fox jumps over the lazy dog. 0 1 2 3 4 5 6 7 8 9.**

7 pt
The quick brown fox jumps over the lazy dog. 0 1 2 3 4 5 6 7 8 9. *The quick brown fox jumps over the lazy dog. 0 1 2 3 4 5 6 7 8 9.* **The quick brown fox jumps over the lazy dog. 0 1 2 3 4 5 6 7 8 9.**

8 pt
The quick brown fox jumps over the lazy dog. 0 1 2 3 4 5 6 7 8 9. *The quick brown fox jumps over the lazy dog. 0 1 2 3 4 5 6 7 8 9.* **The quick brown fox jumps over the lazy dog. 0 1 2 3 4 5 6 7 8 9.**

9 pt
The quick brown fox jumps over the lazy dog. 0 1 2 3 4 5 6 7 8 9. *The quick brown fox jumps over the lazy dog. 0 1 2 3 4 5 6 7 8 9.* **The quick brown fox jumps over the lazy dog. 0 1 2 3 4 5 6 7 8 9.**

10 pt
The quick brown fox jumps over the lazy dog. 0 1 2 3 4 5 6 7 8 9. *The quick brown fox jumps over the lazy dog. 0 1 2 3 4 5 6 7 8 9.* **The quick brown fox jumps over the lazy dog. 0 1 2 3 4 5 6 7 8 9.**

12 pt
The quick brown fox jumps over the lazy dog. 0 1 2 3 4 5 6 7 8 9. *The quick brown fox jumps over the lazy dog. 0 1 2 3 4 5 6 7 8 9.* **The quick brown fox jumps over the lazy dog. 0 1 2 3 4 5 6 7 8 9.**

14 pt
The quick brown fox jumps over the lazy dog. 0 1 2 3 4 5 6 7 8 9. *The quick brown fox jumps over the lazy dog. 0 1 2 3 4 5 6 7 8 9.* **The quick brown fox jumps over the lazy dog. 0 1 2 3 4 5 6 7 8 9.**

Black: 25% Tint
HEX #C7C8CA

6 pt
The quick brown fox jumps over the lazy dog. 0 1 2 3 4 5 6 7 8 9. *The quick brown fox jumps over the lazy dog. 0 1 2 3 4 5 6 7 8 9.* **The quick brown fox jumps over the lazy dog. 0 1 2 3 4 5 6 7 8 9.**

7 pt
The quick brown fox jumps over the lazy dog. 0 1 2 3 4 5 6 7 8 9. *The quick brown fox jumps over the lazy dog. 0 1 2 3 4 5 6 7 8 9.* **The quick brown fox jumps over the lazy dog. 0 1 2 3 4 5 6 7 8 9.**

8 pt
The quick brown fox jumps over the lazy dog. 0 1 2 3 4 5 6 7 8 9. *The quick brown fox jumps over the lazy dog. 0 1 2 3 4 5 6 7 8 9.* **The quick brown fox jumps over the lazy dog. 0 1 2 3 4 5 6 7 8 9.**

9 pt
The quick brown fox jumps over the lazy dog. 0 1 2 3 4 5 6 7 8 9. *The quick brown fox jumps over the lazy dog. 0 1 2 3 4 5 6 7 8 9.* **The quick brown fox jumps over the lazy dog. 0 1 2 3 4 5 6 7 8 9.**

10 pt
The quick brown fox jumps over the lazy dog. 0 1 2 3 4 5 6 7 8 9. *The quick brown fox jumps over the lazy dog. 0 1 2 3 4 5 6 7 8 9.* **The quick brown fox jumps over the lazy dog. 0 1 2 3 4 5 6 7 8 9.**

12 pt
The quick brown fox jumps over the lazy dog. 0 1 2 3 4 5 6 7 8 9. *The quick brown fox jumps over the lazy dog. 0 1 2 3 4 5 6 7 8 9.* **The quick brown fox jumps over the lazy dog. 0 1 2 3 4 5 6 7 8 9.**

14 pt
The quick brown fox jumps over the lazy dog. 0 1 2 3 4 5 6 7 8 9. *The quick brown fox jumps over the lazy dog. 0 1 2 3 4 5 6 7 8 9.* **The quick brown fox jumps over the lazy dog. 0 1 2 3 4 5 6 7 8 9.**

Black: 10% Tint
HEX #E6E7E8

6 pt
The quick brown fox jumps over the lazy dog. 0 1 2 3 4 5 6 7 8 9. *The quick brown fox jumps over the lazy dog. 0 1 2 3 4 5 6 7 8 9.* **The quick brown fox jumps over the lazy dog. 0 1 2 3 4 5 6 7 8 9.**

7 pt
The quick brown fox jumps over the lazy dog. 0 1 2 3 4 5 6 7 8 9. *The quick brown fox jumps over the lazy dog. 0 1 2 3 4 5 6 7 8 9.* **The quick brown fox jumps over the lazy dog. 0 1 2 3 4 5 6 7 8 9.**

8 pt
The quick brown fox jumps over the lazy dog. 0 1 2 3 4 5 6 7 8 9. *The quick brown fox jumps over the lazy dog. 0 1 2 3 4 5 6 7 8 9.* **The quick brown fox jumps over the lazy dog. 0 1 2 3 4 5 6 7 8 9.**

9 pt
The quick brown fox jumps over the lazy dog. 0 1 2 3 4 5 6 7 8 9. *The quick brown fox jumps over the lazy dog. 0 1 2 3 4 5 6 7 8 9.* **The quick brown fox jumps over the lazy dog. 0 1 2 3 4 5 6 7 8 9.**

10 pt
The quick brown fox jumps over the lazy dog. 0 1 2 3 4 5 6 7 8 9. *The quick brown fox jumps over the lazy dog. 0 1 2 3 4 5 6 7 8 9.* **The quick brown fox jumps over the lazy dog. 0 1 2 3 4 5 6 7 8 9.**

12 pt
The quick brown fox jumps over the lazy dog. 0 1 2 3 4 5 6 7 8 9. *The quick brown fox jumps over the lazy dog. 0 1 2 3 4 5 6 7 8 9.* **The quick brown fox jumps over the lazy dog. 0 1 2 3 4 5 6 7 8 9.**

14 pt
The quick brown fox jumps over the lazy dog. 0 1 2 3 4 5 6 7 8 9. *The quick brown fox jumps over the lazy dog. 0 1 2 3 4 5 6 7 8 9.* **The quick brown fox jumps over the lazy dog. 0 1 2 3 4 5 6 7 8 9.**

COURIER

4 pt

The quick brown fox jumps over the lazy dog. 0 1 2 3 4 5 6 7 8 9. *The quick brown fox jumps over the lazy dog. 0 1 2 3 4 5 6 7 8 9.* **The quick brown fox jumps over the lazy dog. 0 1 2 3 4 5 6 7 8 9.**

5 pt

The quick brown fox jumps over the lazy dog. 0 1 2 3 4 5 6 7 8 9. *The quick brown fox jumps over the lazy dog. 0 1 2 3 4 5 6 7 8 9.* **The quick brown fox jumps over the lazy dog. 0 1 2 3 4 5 6 7 8 9.**

6 pt

The quick brown fox jumps over the lazy dog. 0 1 2 3 4 5 6 7 8 9. *The quick brown fox jumps over the lazy dog. 0 1 2 3 4 5 6 7 8 9.* **The quick brown fox jumps over the lazy dog. 0 1 2 3 4 5 6 7 8 9.**

7 pt

The quick brown fox jumps over the lazy dog. 0 1 2 3 4 5 6 7 8 9. *The quick brown fox jumps over the lazy dog. 0 1 2 3 4 5 6 7 8 9.* **The quick brown fox jumps over the lazy dog. 0 1 2 3 4 5 6 7 8 9.**

8 pt

The quick brown fox jumps over the lazy dog. 0 1 2 3 4 5 6 7 8 9. *The quick brown fox jumps over the lazy dog. 0 1 2 3 4 5 6 7 8 9.* **The quick brown fox jumps over the lazy dog. 0 1 2 3 4 5 6 7 8 9.**

9 pt

The quick brown fox jumps over the lazy dog. 0 1 2 3 4 5 6 7 8 9. *The quick brown fox jumps over the lazy dog. 0 1 2 3 4 5 6 7 8 9.* **The quick brown fox jumps over the lazy dog. 0 1 2 3 4 5 6 7 8 9.**

10 pt

The quick brown fox jumps over the lazy dog. 0 1 2 3 4 5 6 7 8 9. *The quick brown fox jumps over the lazy dog. 0 1 2 3 4 5 6 7 8 9.* **The quick brown fox jumps over the lazy dog. 0 1 2 3 4 5 6 7 8 9.**

12 pt

The quick brown fox jumps over the lazy dog. 0 1 2 3 4 5 6 7 8 9. *The quick brown fox jumps over the lazy dog. 0 1 2 3 4 5 6 7 8 9.* **The quick brown fox jumps over the lazy dog. 0 1 2 3 4 5 6 7 8 9.**

14 pt

The quick brown fox jumps over the lazy dog. 0 1 2 3 4 5 6 7 8 9. *The quick brown fox jumps over the lazy dog. 0 1 2 3 4 5 6 7 8 9.* **The quick brown fox jumps over the lazy dog. 0 1 2 3 4 5 6 7 8 9.**

16 pt

The quick brown fox jumps over the lazy

dog. 0 1 2 3 4 5 6 7 8 9. *The quick brown fox jumps over the lazy dog. 0 1 2 3 4 5 6 7 8 9.* **The quick brown fox jumps over the lazy dog. 0 1 2 3 4 5 6 7 8 9.**

18 pt

The quick brown fox jumps over the lazy dog. 0 1 2 3 4 5 6 7 8 9. *The quick brown fox jumps over the lazy dog. 0 1 2 3 4 5 6 7 8 9.* **The quick brown fox jumps over the lazy dog. 0 1 2 3 4 5 6 7 8 9.**

24 pt

The quick brown fox jumps over the lazy dog. 0 1 2 3 4 5 6 7 8 9. *The quick brown fox jumps over the lazy dog. 0 1 2 3 4 5 6 7 8 9.* **The quick brown fox jumps over the lazy dog. 0 1 2 3 4 5 6 7 8 9.**

36 pt

The quick brown fox jumps over the lazy dog. 0 1

Black: 75% Tint
HEX #636466

6 pt
The quick brown fox jumps over the lazy dog. 0 1 2 3 4 5 6 7 8 9. *The quick brown fox jumps over the lazy dog. 0 1 2 3 4 5 6 7 8 9.* **The quick brown fox jumps over the lazy dog. 0 1 2 3 4 5 6 7 8 9.**

7 pt
The quick brown fox jumps over the lazy dog. 0 1 2 3 4 5 6 7 8 9. *The quick brown fox jumps over the lazy dog. 0 1 2 3 4 5 6 7 8 9.* **The quick brown fox jumps over the lazy dog. 0 1 2 3 4 5 6 7 8 9.**

8 pt
The quick brown fox jumps over the lazy dog. 0 1 2 3 4 5 6 7 8 9. *The quick brown fox jumps over the lazy dog. 0 1 2 3 4 5 6 7 8 9.* **The quick brown fox jumps over the lazy dog. 0 1 2 3 4 5 6 7 8 9.**

9 pt
The quick brown fox jumps over the lazy dog. 0 1 2 3 4 5 6 7 8 9. *The quick brown fox jumps over the lazy dog. 0 1 2 3 4 5 6 7 8 9.* **The quick brown fox jumps over the lazy dog. 0 1 2 3 4 5 6 7 8 9.**

10 pt
The quick brown fox jumps over the lazy dog. 0 1 2 3 4 5 6 7 8 9. *The quick brown fox jumps over the lazy dog. 0 1 2 3 4 5 6 7 8 9.* **The quick brown fox jumps over the lazy dog. 0 1 2 3 4 5 6 7 8 9.**

12 pt
The quick brown fox jumps over the lazy dog. 0 1 2 3 4 5 6 7 8 9. *The quick brown fox jumps over the lazy dog. 0 1 2 3 4 5 6 7 8 9.* **The quick brown fox jumps over the lazy dog. 0 1 2 3 4 5 6 7 8 9.**

Black: 50% Tint
HEX #939598

6 pt
The quick brown fox jumps over the lazy dog. 0 1 2 3 4 5 6 7 8 9. *The quick brown fox jumps over the lazy dog. 0 1 2 3 4 5 6 7 8 9.* **The quick brown fox jumps over the lazy dog. 0 1 2 3 4 5 6 7 8 9.**

7 pt
The quick brown fox jumps over the lazy dog. 0 1 2 3 4 5 6 7 8 9. *The quick brown fox jumps over the lazy dog. 0 1 2 3 4 5 6 7 8 9.* **The quick brown fox jumps over the lazy dog. 0 1 2 3 4 5 6 7 8 9.**

8 pt
The quick brown fox jumps over the lazy dog. 0 1 2 3 4 5 6 7 8 9. *The quick brown fox jumps over the lazy dog. 0 1 2 3 4 5 6 7 8 9.* **The quick brown fox jumps over the lazy dog. 0 1 2 3 4 5 6 7 8 9.**

9 pt
The quick brown fox jumps over the lazy dog. 0 1 2 3 4 5 6 7 8 9. *The quick brown fox jumps over the lazy dog. 0 1 2 3 4 5 6 7 8 9.* **The quick brown fox jumps over the lazy dog. 0 1 2 3 4 5 6 7 8 9.**

10 pt
The quick brown fox jumps over the lazy dog. 0 1 2 3 4 5 6 7 8 9. *The quick brown fox jumps over the lazy dog. 0 1 2 3 4 5 6 7 8 9.* **The quick brown fox jumps over the lazy dog. 0 1 2 3 4 5 6 7 8 9.**

12 pt
The quick brown fox jumps over the lazy dog. 0 1 2 3 4 5 6 7 8 9. *The quick brown fox jumps over the lazy dog. 0 1 2 3 4 5 6 7 8 9.* **The quick brown fox jumps over the lazy dog. 0 1 2 3 4 5 6 7 8 9.**

Black: 25% Tint
HEX #C7C8CA

6 pt

The quick brown fox jumps over the lazy dog. 0 1 2 3 4 5 6 7 8 9. The quick brown fox jumps over the lazy dog. 0 1 2 3 4 5 6 7 8 9. The quick brown fox jumps over the lazy dog. 0 1 2 3 4 5 6 7 8 9.

7 pt

The quick brown fox jumps over the lazy dog. 0 1 2 3 4 5 6 7 8 9. *The quick brown fox jumps over the lazy dog. 0 1 2 3 4 5 6 7 8 9.* **The quick brown fox jumps over the lazy dog. 0 1 2 3 4 5 6 7 8 9.**

8 pt

The quick brown fox jumps over the lazy dog. 0 1 2 3 4 5 6 7 8 9. *The quick brown fox jumps over the lazy dog. 0 1 2 3 4 5 6 7 8 9.* **The quick brown fox jumps over the lazy dog. 0 1 2 3 4 5 6 7 8 9.**

9 pt

The quick brown fox jumps over the lazy dog. 0 1 2 3 4 5 6 7 8 9. *The quick brown fox jumps over the lazy dog. 0 1 2 3 4 5 6 7 8 9.* The quick brown fox jumps over the lazy dog. 0 1 2 3 4 5 6 7 8 9.

10 pt

The quick brown fox jumps over the lazy dog. 0 1 2 3 4 5 6 7 8 9. *The quick brown fox jumps over the lazy dog. 0 1 2 3 4 5 6 7 8 9.* **The quick brown fox jumps over the lazy dog. 0 1 2 3 4 5 6 7 8 9.**

12 pt

The quick brown fox jumps over the lazy dog. 0 1 2 3 4 5 6 7 8 9. *The quick brown fox jumps over the lazy dog. 0 1 2 3 4 5 6 7 8 9.* **The quick brown fox jumps over the lazy dog. 0 1 2 3 4 5 6 7 8 9.**

Black: 10% Tint
HEX #E6E7E8

6 pt

The quick brown fox jumps over the lazy dog. 0 1 2 3 4 5 6 7 8 9. The quick brown fox jumps over the lazy dog. 0 1 2 3 4 5 6 7 8 9. The quick brown fox jumps over the lazy dog. 0 1 2 3 4 5 6 7 8 9.

7 pt

The quick brown fox jumps over the lazy dog. 0 1 2 3 4 5 6 7 8 9. *The quick brown fox jumps over the lazy dog. 0 1 2 3 4 5 6 7 8 9.* **The quick brown fox jumps over the lazy dog. 0 1 2 3 4 5 6 7 8 9.**

8 pt

The quick brown fox jumps over the lazy dog. 0 1 2 3 4 5 6 7 8 9. *The quick brown fox jumps over the lazy dog. 0 1 2 3 4 5 6 7 8 9.* **The quick brown fox jumps over the lazy dog. 0 1 2 3 4 5 6 7 8 9.**

9 pt

The quick brown fox jumps over the lazy dog. 0 1 2 3 4 5 6 7 8 9. *The quick brown fox jumps over the lazy dog. 0 1 2 3 4 5 6 7 8 9.* The quick brown fox jumps over the lazy dog. 0 1 2 3 4 5 6 7 8 9.

10 pt

The quick brown fox jumps over the lazy dog. 0 1 2 3 4 5 6 7 8 9. *The quick brown fox jumps over the lazy dog. 0 1 2 3 4 5 6 7 8 9.* **The quick brown fox jumps over the lazy dog. 0 1 2 3 4 5 6 7 8 9.**

12 pt

The quick brown fox jumps over the lazy dog. 0 1 2 3 4 5 6 7 8 9. *The quick brown fox jumps over the lazy dog. 0 1 2 3 4 5 6 7 8 9.* **The quick brown fox jumps over the lazy dog. 0 1 2 3 4 5 6 7 8 9.**

DIDOT

4 pt
The quick brown fox jumps over the lazy dog. 0 1 2 3 4 5 6 7 8 9. *The quick brown fox jumps over the lazy dog. 0 1 2 3 4 5 6 7 8 9.* **The quick brown fox jumps over the lazy dog. 0 1 2 3 4 5 6 7 8 9.**

5 pt
The quick brown fox jumps over the lazy dog. 0 1 2 3 4 5 6 7 8 9. *The quick brown fox jumps over the lazy dog. 0 1 2 3 4 5 6 7 8 9.* **The quick brown fox jumps over the lazy dog. 0 1 2 3 4 5 6 7 8 9.**

6 pt
The quick brown fox jumps over the lazy dog. 0 1 2 3 4 5 6 7 8 9. *The quick brown fox jumps over the lazy dog. 0 1 2 3 4 5 6 7 8 9.* **The quick brown fox jumps over the lazy dog. 0 1 2 3 4 5 6 7 8 9.**

7 pt
The quick brown fox jumps over the lazy dog. 0 1 2 3 4 5 6 7 8 9. *The quick brown fox jumps over the lazy dog. 0 1 2 3 4 5 6 7 8 9.* **The quick brown fox jumps over the lazy dog. 0 1 2 3 4 5 6 7 8 9.**

8 pt
The quick brown fox jumps over the lazy dog. 0 1 2 3 4 5 6 7 8 9. *The quick brown fox jumps over the lazy dog. 0 1 2 3 4 5 6 7 8 9.* **The quick brown fox jumps over the lazy dog. 0 1 2 3 4 5 6 7 8 9.**

9 pt
The quick brown fox jumps over the lazy dog. 0 1 2 3 4 5 6 7 8 9. *The quick brown fox jumps over the lazy dog. 0 1 2 3 4 5 6 7 8 9.* **The quick brown fox jumps over the lazy dog. 0 1 2 3 4 5 6 7 8 9.**

10 pt
The quick brown fox jumps over the lazy dog. 0 1 2 3 4 5 6 7 8 9. *The quick brown fox jumps over the lazy dog. 0 1 2 3 4 5 6 7 8 9.* **The quick brown fox jumps over the lazy dog. 0 1 2 3 4 5 6 7 8 9.**

12 pt
The quick brown fox jumps over the lazy dog. 0 1 2 3 4 5 6 7 8 9. *The quick brown fox jumps over the lazy dog. 0 1 2 3 4 5 6 7 8 9.* **The quick brown fox jumps over the lazy dog. 0 1 2 3 4 5 6 7 8 9.**

14 pt
The quick brown fox jumps over the lazy dog. 0 1 2 3 4 5 6 7 8 9. *The quick brown fox jumps over the lazy dog. 0 1 2 3 4 5 6 7 8 9.* **The quick brown fox jumps over the lazy dog. 0 1 2 3 4 5 6 7 8 9.**

16 pt
The quick brown fox jumps over the lazy dog. 0 1 2 3 4 5 6 7 8 9. *The quick brown fox jumps over the lazy dog. 0 1 2 3 4 5 6 7 8 9.* **The quick brown fox jumps over the lazy dog. 0 1 2 3 4 5 6 7 8 9.**

18 pt

The quick brown fox jumps over the lazy dog. 0 1 2 3 4 5 6 7 8 9. *The quick brown fox jumps over the lazy dog. 0 1 2 3 4 5 6 7 8 9.* **The quick brown fox jumps over the lazy dog. 0 1 2 3 4 5 6 7 8 9.**

24 pt

The quick brown fox jumps over the lazy dog. 0 1 2 3 4 5 6 7 8 9. *The quick brown fox jumps over the lazy dog. 0 1 2 3 4 5 6 7 8 9.* **The quick brown fox jumps over the lazy dog. 0 1 2 3 4 5 6 7 8 9.**

36 pt

The quick brown fox jumps over the lazy dog. 0 1 2 3 4 5 6 7 8 9. *The quick brown fox jumps over the lazy dog. 0 1 2 3 4 5 6 7 8 9.* **The quick brown fox**

Black: 75% Tint
HEX #636466

6 pt
The quick brown fox jumps over the lazy dog. 0 1 2 3 4 5 6 7 8 9. *The quick brown fox jumps over the lazy dog. 0 1 2 3 4 5 6 7 8 9.* **The quick brown fox jumps over the lazy dog. 0 1 2 3 4 5 6 7 8 9.**

7 pt
The quick brown fox jumps over the lazy dog. 0 1 2 3 4 5 6 7 8 9. *The quick brown fox jumps over the lazy dog. 0 1 2 3 4 5 6 7 8 9.* **The quick brown fox jumps over the lazy dog. 0 1 2 3 4 5 6 7 8 9.**

8 pt
The quick brown fox jumps over the lazy dog. 0 1 2 3 4 5 6 7 8 9. *The quick brown fox jumps over the lazy dog. 0 1 2 3 4 5 6 7 8 9.* **The quick brown fox jumps over the lazy dog. 0 1 2 3 4 5 6 7 8 9.**

9 pt
The quick brown fox jumps over the lazy dog. 0 1 2 3 4 5 6 7 8 9. *The quick brown fox jumps over the lazy dog. 0 1 2 3 4 5 6 7 8 9.* **The quick brown fox jumps over the lazy dog. 0 1 2 3 4 5 6 7 8 9.**

10 pt
The quick brown fox jumps over the lazy dog. 0 1 2 3 4 5 6 7 8 9. *The quick brown fox jumps over the lazy dog. 0 1 2 3 4 5 6 7 8 9.* **The quick brown fox jumps over the lazy dog. 0 1 2 3 4 5 6 7 8 9.**

12 pt
The quick brown fox jumps over the lazy dog. 0 1 2 3 4 5 6 7 8 9. *The quick brown fox jumps over the lazy dog. 0 1 2 3 4 5 6 7 8 9.* **The quick brown fox jumps over the lazy dog. 0 1 2 3 4 5 6 7 8 9.**

14 pt
The quick brown fox jumps over the lazy dog. 0 1 2 3 4 5 6 7 8 9. *The quick brown fox jumps over the lazy dog. 0 1 2 3 4 5 6 7 8 9.* **The quick brown fox jumps over the lazy dog.**

Black: 50% Tint
HEX #939598

6 pt
The quick brown fox jumps over the lazy dog. 0 1 2 3 4 5 6 7 8 9. *The quick brown fox jumps over the lazy dog. 0 1 2 3 4 5 6 7 8 9.* **The quick brown fox jumps over the lazy dog. 0 1 2 3 4 5 6 7 8 9.**

7 pt
The quick brown fox jumps over the lazy dog. 0 1 2 3 4 5 6 7 8 9. *The quick brown fox jumps over the lazy dog. 0 1 2 3 4 5 6 7 8 9.* **The quick brown fox jumps over the lazy dog. 0 1 2 3 4 5 6 7 8 9.**

8 pt
The quick brown fox jumps over the lazy dog. 0 1 2 3 4 5 6 7 8 9. *The quick brown fox jumps over the lazy dog. 0 1 2 3 4 5 6 7 8 9.* **The quick brown fox jumps over the lazy dog. 0 1 2 3 4 5 6 7 8 9.**

9 pt
The quick brown fox jumps over the lazy dog. 0 1 2 3 4 5 6 7 8 9. *The quick brown fox jumps over the lazy dog. 0 1 2 3 4 5 6 7 8 9.* **The quick brown fox jumps over the lazy dog. 0 1 2 3 4 5 6 7 8 9.**

10 pt
The quick brown fox jumps over the lazy dog. 0 1 2 3 4 5 6 7 8 9. *The quick brown fox jumps over the lazy dog. 0 1 2 3 4 5 6 7 8 9.* **The quick brown fox jumps over the lazy dog. 0 1 2 3 4 5 6 7 8 9.**

12 pt
The quick brown fox jumps over the lazy dog. 0 1 2 3 4 5 6 7 8 9. *The quick brown fox jumps over the lazy dog. 0 1 2 3 4 5 6 7 8 9.* **The quick brown fox jumps over the lazy dog. 0 1 2 3 4 5 6 7 8 9.**

14 pt
The quick brown fox jumps over the lazy dog. 0 1 2 3 4 5 6 7 8 9. *The quick brown fox jumps over the lazy dog. 0 1 2 3 4 5 6 7 8 9.* **The quick brown fox jumps over the lazy dog.**

Black: 25% Tint
HEX #C7C8CA

6 pt
The quick brown fox jumps over the lazy dog. 0 1 2 3 4 5 6 7 8 9. The quick brown fox jumps over the lazy dog. 0 1 2 3 4 5 6 7 8 9. The quick brown fox jumps over the lazy dog. 0 1 2 3 4 5 6 7 8 9.

7 pt
The quick brown fox jumps over the lazy dog. 0 1 2 3 4 5 6 7 8 9. *The quick brown fox jumps over the lazy dog. 0 1 2 3 4 5 6 7 8 9.* **The quick brown fox jumps over the lazy dog. 0 1 2 3 4 5 6 7 8 9.**

8 pt
The quick brown fox jumps over the lazy dog. 0 1 2 3 4 5 6 7 8 9. *The quick brown fox jumps over the lazy dog. 0 1 2 3 4 5 6 7 8 9.* **The quick brown fox jumps over the lazy dog. 0 1 2 3 4 5 6 7 8 9.**

9 pt
The quick brown fox jumps over the lazy dog. 0 1 2 3 4 5 6 7 8 9. *The quick brown fox jumps over the lazy dog. 0 1 2 3 4 5 6 7 8 9.* **The quick brown fox jumps over the lazy dog. 0 1 2 3 4 5 6 7 8 9.**

10 pt
The quick brown fox jumps over the lazy dog. 0 1 2 3 4 5 6 7 8 9. *The quick brown fox jumps over the lazy dog. 0 1 2 3 4 5 6 7 8 9.* **The quick brown fox jumps over the lazy dog. 0 1 2 3 4 5 6 7 8 9.**

12 pt
The quick brown fox jumps over the lazy dog. 0 1 2 3 4 5 6 7 8 9. *The quick brown fox jumps over the lazy dog. 0 1 2 3 4 5 6 7 8 9.* **The quick brown fox jumps over the lazy dog. 0 1 2 3 4 5 6 7 8 9.**

14 pt
The quick brown fox jumps over the lazy dog. 0 1 2 3 4 5 6 7 8 9. *The quick brown fox jumps over the lazy dog. 0 1 2 3* **4 5 6 7 8 9. The quick brown fox jumps over the lazy dog.**

Black: 10% Tint
HEX #E6E7E8

6 pt
The quick brown fox jumps over the lazy dog. 0 1 2 3 4 5 6 7 8 9. The quick brown fox jumps over the lazy dog. 0 1 2 3 4 5 6 7 8 9. The quick brown fox jumps over the lazy dog. 0 1 2 3 4 5 6 7 8 9.

7 pt
The quick brown fox jumps over the lazy dog. 0 1 2 3 4 5 6 7 8 9. *The quick brown fox jumps over the lazy dog. 0 1 2 3 4 5 6 7 8 9.* **The quick brown fox jumps over the lazy dog. 0 1 2 3 4 5 6 7 8 9.**

8 pt
The quick brown fox jumps over the lazy dog. 0 1 2 3 4 5 6 7 8 9. *The quick brown fox jumps over the lazy dog. 0 1 2 3 4 5 6 7 8 9.* **The quick brown fox jumps over the lazy dog. 0 1 2 3 4 5 6 7 8 9.**

9 pt
The quick brown fox jumps over the lazy dog. 0 1 2 3 4 5 6 7 8 9. *The quick brown fox jumps over the lazy dog. 0 1 2 3 4 5 6 7 8 9.* **The quick brown fox jumps over the lazy dog. 0 1 2 3 4 5 6 7 8 9.**

10 pt
The quick brown fox jumps over the lazy dog. 0 1 2 3 4 5 6 7 8 9. *The quick brown fox jumps over the lazy dog. 0 1 2 3 4 5 6 7 8 9.* **The quick brown fox jumps over the lazy dog. 0 1 2 3 4 5 6 7 8 9.**

12 pt
The quick brown fox jumps over the lazy dog. 0 1 2 3 4 5 6 7 8 9. *The quick brown fox jumps over the lazy dog. 0 1 2 3 4 5 6 7 8 9.* **The quick brown fox jumps over the lazy dog. 0 1 2 3 4 5 6 7 8 9.**

14 pt
The quick brown fox jumps over the lazy dog. 0 1 2 3 4 5 6 7 8 9. *The quick brown fox jumps over the lazy dog. 0 1 2 3* **4 5 6 7 8 9. The quick brown fox jumps over the lazy dog.**

PALATINO

4 pt
The quick brown fox jumps over the lazy dog. 0 1 2 3 4 5 6 7 8 9. *The quick brown fox jumps over the lazy dog. 0 1 2 3 4 5 6 7 8 9.* **The quick brown fox jumps over the lazy dog. 0 1 2 3 4 5 6 7 8 9.**

5 pt
The quick brown fox jumps over the lazy dog. 0 1 2 3 4 5 6 7 8 9. *The quick brown fox jumps over the lazy dog. 0 1 2 3 4 5 6 7 8 9.* **The quick brown fox jumps over the lazy dog. 0 1 2 3 4 5 6 7 8 9.**

6 pt
The quick brown fox jumps over the lazy dog. 0 1 2 3 4 5 6 7 8 9. *The quick brown fox jumps over the lazy dog. 0 1 2 3 4 5 6 7 8 9.* **The quick brown fox jumps over the lazy dog. 0 1 2 3 4 5 6 7 8 9.**

7 pt
The quick brown fox jumps over the lazy dog. 0 1 2 3 4 5 6 7 8 9. *The quick brown fox jumps over the lazy dog. 0 1 2 3 4 5 6 7 8 9.* **The quick brown fox jumps over the lazy dog. 0 1 2 3 4 5 6 7 8 9.**

8 pt
The quick brown fox jumps over the lazy dog. 0 1 2 3 4 5 6 7 8 9. *The quick brown fox jumps over the lazy dog. 0 1 2 3 4 5 6 7 8 9.* **The quick brown fox jumps over the lazy dog. 0 1 2 3 4 5 6 7 8 9.**

9 pt
The quick brown fox jumps over the lazy dog. 0 1 2 3 4 5 6 7 8 9. *The quick brown fox jumps over the lazy dog. 0 1 2 3 4 5 6 7 8 9.* **The quick brown fox jumps over the lazy dog. 0 1 2 3 4 5 6 7 8 9.**

10 pt
The quick brown fox jumps over the lazy dog. 0 1 2 3 4 5 6 7 8 9. *The quick brown fox jumps over the lazy dog. 0 1 2 3 4 5 6 7 8 9.* **The quick brown fox jumps over the lazy dog. 0 1 2 3 4 5 6 7 8 9.**

12 pt
The quick brown fox jumps over the lazy dog. 0 1 2 3 4 5 6 7 8 9. *The quick brown fox jumps over the lazy dog. 0 1 2 3 4 5 6 7 8 9.* **The quick brown fox jumps over the lazy dog. 0 1 2 3 4 5 6 7 8 9.**

14 pt
The quick brown fox jumps over the lazy dog. 0 1 2 3 4 5 6 7 8 9. *The quick brown fox jumps over the lazy dog. 0 1 2 3 4 5 6 7 8 9.* **The quick brown fox jumps over the lazy dog. 0 1 2 3 4 5 6 7 8 9.**

16 pt
The quick brown fox jumps over the lazy dog. 0 1 2 3 4 5 6 7 8 9. *The quick brown fox jumps over the lazy dog. 0 1 2 3 4 5 6 7 8 9.* **The quick brown fox jumps over the lazy dog. 0 1 2 3 4 5 6 7 8 9.**

18 pt

The quick brown fox jumps over the lazy dog. 0 1 2 3 4 5 6 7 8 9. *The quick brown fox jumps over the lazy dog. 0 1 2 3 4 5 6 7 8 9.* **The quick brown fox jumps over the lazy dog. 0 1 2 3 4 5 6 7 8 9.**

24 pt

The quick brown fox jumps over the lazy dog. 0 1 2 3 4 5 6 7 8 9. *The quick brown fox jumps over the lazy dog. 0 1 2 3 4 5 6 7 8 9.* **The quick brown fox jumps over the lazy dog. 0 1 2 3 4 5 6 7 8 9.**

36 pt

The quick brown fox jumps over the lazy dog. 0 1 2 3 4 5 6 7 8 9. *The quick brown fox jumps over the lazy dog. 0 1 2 3 4 5 6 7 8 9.* **The quick brown fox jumps over the lazy**

Black: 75% Tint
HEX #636466

6 pt
The quick brown fox jumps over the lazy dog. 0 1 2 3 4 5 6 7 8 9. *The quick brown fox jumps over the lazy dog. 0 1 2 3 4 5 6 7 8 9.* **The quick brown fox jumps over the lazy dog. 0 1 2 3 4 5 6 7 8 9.**

7 pt
The quick brown fox jumps over the lazy dog. 0 1 2 3 4 5 6 7 8 9. *The quick brown fox jumps over the lazy dog. 0 1 2 3 4 5 6 7 8 9.* **The quick brown fox jumps over the lazy dog. 0 1 2 3 4 5 6 7 8 9.**

8 pt
The quick brown fox jumps over the lazy dog. 0 1 2 3 4 5 6 7 8 9. *The quick brown fox jumps over the lazy dog. 0 1 2 3 4 5 6 7 8 9.* **The quick brown fox jumps over the lazy dog. 0 1 2 3 4 5 6 7 8 9.**

9 pt
The quick brown fox jumps over the lazy dog. 0 1 2 3 4 5 6 7 8 9. *The quick brown fox jumps over the lazy dog. 0 1 2 3 4 5 6 7 8 9.* **The quick brown fox jumps over the lazy dog. 0 1 2 3 4 5 6 7 8 9.**

10 pt
The quick brown fox jumps over the lazy dog. 0 1 2 3 4 5 6 7 8 9. *The quick brown fox jumps over the lazy dog. 0 1 2 3 4 5 6 7 8 9.* **The quick brown fox jumps over the lazy dog. 0 1 2 3 4 5 6 7 8 9.**

12 pt
The quick brown fox jumps over the lazy dog. 0 1 2 3 4 5 6 7 8 9. *The quick brown fox jumps over the lazy dog. 0 1 2 3 4 5 6 7 8 9.* **The quick brown fox jumps over the lazy dog. 0 1 2 3 4 5 6 7 8 9.**

14 pt
The quick brown fox jumps over the lazy dog. 0 1 2 3 4 5 6 7 8 9. *The quick brown fox jumps over the lazy dog. 0 1 2 3 4 5 6 7 8 9.* **The quick brown fox jumps over the lazy dog.**

Black: 50% Tint
HEX #939598

6 pt
The quick brown fox jumps over the lazy dog. 0 1 2 3 4 5 6 7 8 9. *The quick brown fox jumps over the lazy dog. 0 1 2 3 4 5 6 7 8 9.* **The quick brown fox jumps over the lazy dog. 0 1 2 3 4 5 6 7 8 9.**

7 pt
The quick brown fox jumps over the lazy dog. 0 1 2 3 4 5 6 7 8 9. *The quick brown fox jumps over the lazy dog. 0 1 2 3 4 5 6 7 8 9.* **The quick brown fox jumps over the lazy dog. 0 1 2 3 4 5 6 7 8 9.**

8 pt
The quick brown fox jumps over the lazy dog. 0 1 2 3 4 5 6 7 8 9. *The quick brown fox jumps over the lazy dog. 0 1 2 3 4 5 6 7 8 9.* **The quick brown fox jumps over the lazy dog. 0 1 2 3 4 5 6 7 8 9.**

9 pt
The quick brown fox jumps over the lazy dog. 0 1 2 3 4 5 6 7 8 9. *The quick brown fox jumps over the lazy dog. 0 1 2 3 4 5 6 7 8 9.* **The quick brown fox jumps over the lazy dog. 0 1 2 3 4 5 6 7 8 9.**

10 pt
The quick brown fox jumps over the lazy dog. 0 1 2 3 4 5 6 7 8 9. *The quick brown fox jumps over the lazy dog. 0 1 2 3 4 5 6 7 8 9.* **The quick brown fox jumps over the lazy dog. 0 1 2 3 4 5 6 7 8 9.**

12 pt
The quick brown fox jumps over the lazy dog. 0 1 2 3 4 5 6 7 8 9. *The quick brown fox jumps over the lazy dog. 0 1 2 3 4 5 6 7 8 9.* **The quick brown fox jumps over the lazy dog. 0 1 2 3 4 5 6 7 8 9.**

14 pt
The quick brown fox jumps over the lazy dog. 0 1 2 3 4 5 6 7 8 9. *The quick brown fox jumps over the lazy dog. 0 1 2 3 4 5 6 7 8 9.* **The quick brown fox jumps over the lazy dog.**

Black: 25% Tint
HEX # C7C8CA

6 pt
The quick brown fox jumps over the lazy dog. 0 1 2 3 4 5 6 7 8 9. *The quick brown fox jumps over the lazy dog. 0 1 2 3 4 5 6 7 8 9.* **The quick brown fox jumps over the lazy dog. 0 1 2 3 4 5 6 7 8 9.**

7 pt
The quick brown fox jumps over the lazy dog. 0 1 2 3 4 5 6 7 8 9. *The quick brown fox jumps over the lazy dog. 0 1 2 3 4 5 6 7 8 9.* **The quick brown fox jumps over the lazy dog. 0 1 2 3 4 5 6 7 8 9.**

8 pt
The quick brown fox jumps over the lazy dog. 0 1 2 3 4 5 6 7 8 9. *The quick brown fox jumps over the lazy dog. 0 1 2 3 4 5 6 7 8 9.* **The quick brown fox jumps over the lazy dog. 0 1 2 3 4 5 6 7 8 9.**

9 pt
The quick brown fox jumps over the lazy dog. 0 1 2 3 4 5 6 7 8 9. *The quick brown fox jumps over the lazy dog. 0 1 2 3 4 5 6 7 8 9.* **The quick brown fox jumps over the lazy dog. 0 1 2 3 4 5 6 7 8 9.**

10 pt
The quick brown fox jumps over the lazy dog. 0 1 2 3 4 5 6 7 8 9. *The quick brown fox jumps over the lazy dog. 0 1 2 3 4 5 6 7 8 9.* **The quick brown fox jumps over the lazy dog. 0 1 2 3 4 5 6 7 8 9.**

12 pt
The quick brown fox jumps over the lazy dog. 0 1 2 3 4 5 6 7 8 9. *The quick brown fox jumps over the lazy dog. 0 1 2 3 4 5 6 7 8 9.* **The quick brown fox jumps over the lazy dog. 0 1 2 3 4 5 6 7 8 9.**

14 pt
The quick brown fox jumps over the lazy dog. 0 1 2 3 4 5 6 7 8 9. *The quick brown fox jumps over the lazy dog. 0 1 2 3 4 5 6 7 8 9.* **The quick brown fox jumps over the lazy dog.**

Black: 10% Tint
HEX # E6E7E8

6 pt
The quick brown fox jumps over the lazy dog. 0 1 2 3 4 5 6 7 8 9. *The quick brown fox jumps over the lazy dog. 0 1 2 3 4 5 6 7 8 9.* **The quick brown fox jumps over the lazy dog. 0 1 2 3 4 5 6 7 8 9.**

7 pt
The quick brown fox jumps over the lazy dog. 0 1 2 3 4 5 6 7 8 9. *The quick brown fox jumps over the lazy dog. 0 1 2 3 4 5 6 7 8 9.* **The quick brown fox jumps over the lazy dog. 0 1 2 3 4 5 6 7 8 9.**

8 pt
The quick brown fox jumps over the lazy dog. 0 1 2 3 4 5 6 7 8 9. *The quick brown fox jumps over the lazy dog. 0 1 2 3 4 5 6 7 8 9.* **The quick brown fox jumps over the lazy dog. 0 1 2 3 4 5 6 7 8 9.**

9 pt
The quick brown fox jumps over the lazy dog. 0 1 2 3 4 5 6 7 8 9. *The quick brown fox jumps over the lazy dog. 0 1 2 3 4 5 6 7 8 9.* **The quick brown fox jumps over the lazy dog. 0 1 2 3 4 5 6 7 8 9.**

10 pt
The quick brown fox jumps over the lazy dog. 0 1 2 3 4 5 6 7 8 9. *The quick brown fox jumps over the lazy dog. 0 1 2 3 4 5 6 7 8 9.* **The quick brown fox jumps over the lazy dog. 0 1 2 3 4 5 6 7 8 9.**

12 pt
The quick brown fox jumps over the lazy dog. 0 1 2 3 4 5 6 7 8 9. *The quick brown fox jumps over the lazy dog. 0 1 2 3 4 5 6 7 8 9.* **The quick brown fox jumps over the lazy dog. 0 1 2 3 4 5 6 7 8 9.**

14 pt
The quick brown fox jumps over the lazy dog. 0 1 2 3 4 5 6 7 8 9. *The quick brown fox jumps over the lazy dog. 0 1 2 3 4 5 6 7 8 9.* **The quick brown fox jumps over the lazy dog.**

TIMES NEW ROMAN

4 pt
The quick brown fox jumps over the lazy dog. 0 1 2 3 4 5 6 7 8 9. *The quick brown fox jumps over the lazy dog. 0 1 2 3 4 5 6 7 8 9.* **The quick brown fox jumps over the lazy dog. 0 1 2 3 4 5 6 7 8 9.**

5 pt
The quick brown fox jumps over the lazy dog. 0 1 2 3 4 5 6 7 8 9. *The quick brown fox jumps over the lazy dog. 0 1 2 3 4 5 6 7 8 9.* **The quick brown fox jumps over the lazy dog. 0 1 2 3 4 5 6 7 8 9.**

6 pt
The quick brown fox jumps over the lazy dog. 0 1 2 3 4 5 6 7 8 9. *The quick brown fox jumps over the lazy dog. 0 1 2 3 4 5 6 7 8 9.* **The quick brown fox jumps over the lazy dog. 0 1 2 3 4 5 6 7 8 9.**

7 pt
The quick brown fox jumps over the lazy dog. 0 1 2 3 4 5 6 7 8 9. *The quick brown fox jumps over the lazy dog. 0 1 2 3 4 5 6 7 8 9.* **The quick brown fox jumps over the lazy dog. 0 1 2 3 4 5 6 7 8 9.**

8 pt
The quick brown fox jumps over the lazy dog. 0 1 2 3 4 5 6 7 8 9. *The quick brown fox jumps over the lazy dog. 0 1 2 3 4 5 6 7 8 9.* **The quick brown fox jumps over the lazy dog. 0 1 2 3 4 5 6 7 8 9.**

9 pt
The quick brown fox jumps over the lazy dog. 0 1 2 3 4 5 6 7 8 9. *The quick brown fox jumps over the lazy dog. 0 1 2 3 4 5 6 7 8 9.* **The quick brown fox jumps over the lazy dog. 0 1 2 3 4 5 6 7 8 9.**

10 pt
The quick brown fox jumps over the lazy dog. 0 1 2 3 4 5 6 7 8 9. *The quick brown fox jumps over the lazy dog. 0 1 2 3 4 5 6 7 8 9.* **The quick brown fox jumps over the lazy dog. 0 1 2 3 4 5 6 7 8 9.**

12 pt
The quick brown fox jumps over the lazy dog. 0 1 2 3 4 5 6 7 8 9. *The quick brown fox jumps over the lazy dog. 0 1 2 3 4 5 6 7 8 9.* **The quick brown fox jumps over the lazy dog. 0 1 2 3 4 5 6 7 8 9.**

14 pt
The quick brown fox jumps over the lazy dog. 0 1 2 3 4 5 6 7 8 9. *The quick brown fox jumps over the lazy dog. 0 1 2 3 4 5 6 7 8 9.* **The quick brown fox jumps over the lazy dog. 0 1 2 3 4 5 6 7 8 9.**

16 pt
The quick brown fox jumps over the lazy dog. 0 1 2 3 4 5 6 7 8 9. *The quick brown fox jumps over the lazy dog. 0 1 2 3 4 5 6 7 8 9.* **The quick brown fox jumps over the lazy dog. 0 1 2 3 4 5 6 7 8 9.**

18 pt

The quick brown fox jumps over the lazy dog. 0 1 2 3 4 5 6 7 8 9. *The quick brown fox jumps over the lazy dog. 0 1 2 3 4 5 6 7 8 9.* **The quick brown fox jumps over the lazy dog. 0 1 2 3 4 5 6 7 8 9.**

24 pt

The quick brown fox jumps over the lazy dog. 0 1 2 3 4 5 6 7 8 9. *The quick brown fox jumps over the lazy dog. 0 1 2 3 4 5 6 7 8 9.* **The quick brown fox jumps over the lazy dog. 0 1 2 3 4 5 6 7 8 9.**

36 pt

The quick brown fox jumps over the lazy dog. 0 1 2 3 4 5 6 7 8 9. *The quick brown fox jumps over the lazy dog. 0 1 2 3 4 5 6 7 8 9.* **The quick brown fox jumps over the lazy dog. 0 1 2 3 4 5**

Black: 75% Tint
HEX #636466

6 pt
The quick brown fox jumps over the lazy dog. 0 1 2 3 4 5 6 7 8 9. *The quick brown fox jumps over the lazy dog. 0 1 2 3 4 5 6 7 8 9.* **The quick brown fox jumps over the lazy dog. 0 1 2 3 4 5 6 7 8 9.**

7 pt
The quick brown fox jumps over the lazy dog. 0 1 2 3 4 5 6 7 8 9. *The quick brown fox jumps over the lazy dog. 0 1 2 3 4 5 6 7 8 9.* **The quick brown fox jumps over the lazy dog. 0 1 2 3 4 5 6 7 8 9.**

8 pt
The quick brown fox jumps over the lazy dog. 0 1 2 3 4 5 6 7 8 9. *The quick brown fox jumps over the lazy dog. 0 1 2 3 4 5 6 7 8 9.* **The quick brown fox jumps over the lazy dog. 0 1 2 3 4 5 6 7 8 9.**

9 pt
The quick brown fox jumps over the lazy dog. 0 1 2 3 4 5 6 7 8 9. *The quick brown fox jumps over the lazy dog. 0 1 2 3 4 5 6 7 8 9.* **The quick brown fox jumps over the lazy dog. 0 1 2 3 4 5 6 7 8 9.**

10 pt
The quick brown fox jumps over the lazy dog. 0 1 2 3 4 5 6 7 8 9. *The quick brown fox jumps over the lazy dog. 0 1 2 3 4 5 6 7 8 9.* **The quick brown fox jumps over the lazy dog. 0 1 2 3 4 5 6 7 8 9.**

12 pt
The quick brown fox jumps over the lazy dog. 0 1 2 3 4 5 6 7 8 9. *The quick brown fox jumps over the lazy dog. 0 1 2 3 4 5 6 7 8 9.* **The quick brown fox jumps over the lazy dog. 0 1 2 3 4 5 6 7 8 9.**

14 pt
The quick brown fox jumps over the lazy dog. 0 1 2 3 4 5 6 7 8 9. *The quick brown fox jumps over the lazy dog. 0 1 2 3 4 5 6 7 8 9.* **The quick brown fox jumps over the lazy dog. 0 1 2 3 4 5 6 7 8 9.**

Black: 50% Tint
HEX #939598

6 pt
The quick brown fox jumps over the lazy dog. 0 1 2 3 4 5 6 7 8 9. *The quick brown fox jumps over the lazy dog. 0 1 2 3 4 5 6 7 8 9.* **The quick brown fox jumps over the lazy dog. 0 1 2 3 4 5 6 7 8 9.**

7 pt
The quick brown fox jumps over the lazy dog. 0 1 2 3 4 5 6 7 8 9. *The quick brown fox jumps over the lazy dog. 0 1 2 3 4 5 6 7 8 9.* **The quick brown fox jumps over the lazy dog. 0 1 2 3 4 5 6 7 8 9.**

8 pt
The quick brown fox jumps over the lazy dog. 0 1 2 3 4 5 6 7 8 9. *The quick brown fox jumps over the lazy dog. 0 1 2 3 4 5 6 7 8 9.* **The quick brown fox jumps over the lazy dog. 0 1 2 3 4 5 6 7 8 9.**

9 pt
The quick brown fox jumps over the lazy dog. 0 1 2 3 4 5 6 7 8 9. *The quick brown fox jumps over the lazy dog. 0 1 2 3 4 5 6 7 8 9.* **The quick brown fox jumps over the lazy dog. 0 1 2 3 4 5 6 7 8 9.**

10 pt
The quick brown fox jumps over the lazy dog. 0 1 2 3 4 5 6 7 8 9. *The quick brown fox jumps over the lazy dog. 0 1 2 3 4 5 6 7 8 9.* **The quick brown fox jumps over the lazy dog. 0 1 2 3 4 5 6 7 8 9.**

12 pt
The quick brown fox jumps over the lazy dog. 0 1 2 3 4 5 6 7 8 9. *The quick brown fox jumps over the lazy dog. 0 1 2 3 4 5 6 7 8 9.* **The quick brown fox jumps over the lazy dog. 0 1 2 3 4 5 6 7 8 9.**

14 pt
The quick brown fox jumps over the lazy dog. 0 1 2 3 4 5 6 7 8 9. *The quick brown fox jumps over the lazy dog. 0 1 2 3 4 5 6 7 8 9.* **The quick brown fox jumps over the lazy dog. 0 1 2 3 4 5 6 7 8 9.**

Black: 25% Tint
HEX #C7C8CA

6 pt
The quick brown fox jumps over the lazy dog. 0 1 2 3 4 5 6 7 8 9. *The quick brown fox jumps over the lazy dog. 0 1 2 3 4 5 6 7 8 9.* **The quick brown fox jumps over the lazy dog. 0 1 2 3 4 5 6 7 8 9.**

7 pt
The quick brown fox jumps over the lazy dog. 0 1 2 3 4 5 6 7 8 9. *The quick brown fox jumps over the lazy dog. 0 1 2 3 4 5 6 7 8 9.* **The quick brown fox jumps over the lazy dog. 0 1 2 3 4 5 6 7 8 9.**

8 pt
The quick brown fox jumps over the lazy dog. 0 1 2 3 4 5 6 7 8 9. *The quick brown fox jumps over the lazy dog. 0 1 2 3 4 5 6 7 8 9.* **The quick brown fox jumps over the lazy dog. 0 1 2 3 4 5 6 7 8 9.**

9 pt
The quick brown fox jumps over the lazy dog. 0 1 2 3 4 5 6 7 8 9. *The quick brown fox jumps over the lazy dog. 0 1 2 3 4 5 6 7 8 9.* **The quick brown fox jumps over the lazy dog. 0 1 2 3 4 5 6 7 8 9.**

10 pt
The quick brown fox jumps over the lazy dog. 0 1 2 3 4 5 6 7 8 9. *The quick brown fox jumps over the lazy dog. 0 1 2 3 4 5 6 7 8 9.* **The quick brown fox jumps over the lazy dog. 0 1 2 3 4 5 6 7 8 9.**

12 pt
The quick brown fox jumps over the lazy dog. 0 1 2 3 4 5 6 7 8 9. *The quick brown fox jumps over the lazy dog. 0 1 2 3 4 5 6 7 8 9.* **The quick brown fox jumps over the lazy dog. 0 1 2 3 4 5 6 7 8 9.**

14 pt
The quick brown fox jumps over the lazy dog. 0 1 2 3 4 5 6 7 8 9. *The quick brown fox jumps over the lazy dog. 0 1 2 3 4 5 6 7 8 9.* **The quick brown fox jumps over the lazy dog. 0 1 2 3 4 5 6 7 8 9.**

Black: 10% Tint
HEX #E6E7E8

6 pt
The quick brown fox jumps over the lazy dog. 0 1 2 3 4 5 6 7 8 9. *The quick brown fox jumps over the lazy dog. 0 1 2 3 4 5 6 7 8 9.* **The quick brown fox jumps over the lazy dog. 0 1 2 3 4 5 6 7 8 9.**

7 pt
The quick brown fox jumps over the lazy dog. 0 1 2 3 4 5 6 7 8 9. *The quick brown fox jumps over the lazy dog. 0 1 2 3 4 5 6 7 8 9.* **The quick brown fox jumps over the lazy dog. 0 1 2 3 4 5 6 7 8 9.**

8 pt
The quick brown fox jumps over the lazy dog. 0 1 2 3 4 5 6 7 8 9. *The quick brown fox jumps over the lazy dog. 0 1 2 3 4 5 6 7 8 9.* **The quick brown fox jumps over the lazy dog. 0 1 2 3 4 5 6 7 8 9.**

9 pt
The quick brown fox jumps over the lazy dog. 0 1 2 3 4 5 6 7 8 9. *The quick brown fox jumps over the lazy dog. 0 1 2 3 4 5 6 7 8 9.* **The quick brown fox jumps over the lazy dog. 0 1 2 3 4 5 6 7 8 9.**

10 pt
The quick brown fox jumps over the lazy dog. 0 1 2 3 4 5 6 7 8 9. *The quick brown fox jumps over the lazy dog. 0 1 2 3 4 5 6 7 8 9.* **The quick brown fox jumps over the lazy dog. 0 1 2 3 4 5 6 7 8 9.**

12 pt
The quick brown fox jumps over the lazy dog. 0 1 2 3 4 5 6 7 8 9. *The quick brown fox jumps over the lazy dog. 0 1 2 3 4 5 6 7 8 9.* **The quick brown fox jumps over the lazy dog. 0 1 2 3 4 5 6 7 8 9.**

14 pt
The quick brown fox jumps over the lazy dog. 0 1 2 3 4 5 6 7 8 9. *The quick brown fox jumps over the lazy dog. 0 1 2 3 4 5 6 7 8 9.* **The quick brown fox jumps over the lazy dog. 0 1 2 3 4 5 6 7 8 9.**

ARIAL

4 pt
The quick brown fox jumps over the lazy dog. 0 1 2 3 4 5 6 7 8 9. *The quick brown fox jumps over the lazy dog. 0 1 2 3 4 5 6 7 8 9.* **The quick brown fox jumps over the lazy dog. 0 1 2 3 4 5 6 7 8 9.**

5 pt
The quick brown fox jumps over the lazy dog. 0 1 2 3 4 5 6 7 8 9. *The quick brown fox jumps over the lazy dog. 0 1 2 3 4 5 6 7 8 9.* **The quick brown fox jumps over the lazy dog. 0 1 2 3 4 5 6 7 8 9.**

6 pt
The quick brown fox jumps over the lazy dog. 0 1 2 3 4 5 6 7 8 9. *The quick brown fox jumps over the lazy dog. 0 1 2 3 4 5 6 7 8 9.* **The quick brown fox jumps over the lazy dog. 0 1 2 3 4 5 6 7 8 9.**

7 pt
The quick brown fox jumps over the lazy dog. 0 1 2 3 4 5 6 7 8 9. *The quick brown fox jumps over the lazy dog. 0 1 2 3 4 5 6 7 8 9.* **The quick brown fox jumps over the lazy dog. 0 1 2 3 4 5 6 7 8 9.**

8 pt
The quick brown fox jumps over the lazy dog. 0 1 2 3 4 5 6 7 8 9. *The quick brown fox jumps over the lazy dog. 0 1 2 3 4 5 6 7 8 9.* **The quick brown fox jumps over the lazy dog. 0 1 2 3 4 5 6 7 8 9.**

9 pt
The quick brown fox jumps over the lazy dog. 0 1 2 3 4 5 6 7 8 9. *The quick brown fox jumps over the lazy dog. 0 1 2 3 4 5 6 7 8 9.* **The quick brown fox jumps over the lazy dog. 0 1 2 3 4 5 6 7 8 9.**

10 pt
The quick brown fox jumps over the lazy dog. 0 1 2 3 4 5 6 7 8 9. *The quick brown fox jumps over the lazy dog. 0 1 2 3 4 5 6 7 8 9.* **The quick brown fox jumps over the lazy dog. 0 1 2 3 4 5 6 7 8 9.**

12 pt
The quick brown fox jumps over the lazy dog. 0 1 2 3 4 5 6 7 8 9. *The quick brown fox jumps over the lazy dog. 0 1 2 3 4 5 6 7 8 9.* **The quick brown fox jumps over the lazy dog. 0 1 2 3 4 5 6 7 8 9.**

14 pt
The quick brown fox jumps over the lazy dog. 0 1 2 3 4 5 6 7 8 9. *The quick brown fox jumps over the lazy dog. 0 1 2 3 4 5 6 7 8 9.* **The quick brown fox jumps over the lazy dog. 0 1 2 3 4 5 6 7 8 9.**

16 pt
The quick brown fox jumps over the lazy dog. 0 1 2 3 4 5 6 7 8 9. *The quick brown fox jumps over the lazy dog. 0 1 2 3 4 5 6 7 8 9.* **The quick brown fox jumps over the lazy dog. 0 1 2 3 4 5 6 7 8 9.**

18 pt

The quick brown fox jumps over the lazy dog. 0 1 2 3 4 5 6 7 8 9. *The quick brown fox jumps over the lazy dog. 0 1 2 3 4 5 6 7 8 9.* **The quick brown fox jumps over the lazy dog. 0 1 2 3 4 5 6 7 8 9.**

24 pt

The quick brown fox jumps over the lazy dog. 0 1 2 3 4 5 6 7 8 9. *The quick brown fox jumps over the lazy dog. 0 1 2 3 4 5 6 7 8 9.* **The quick brown fox jumps over the lazy dog. 0 1 2 3 4 5 6 7 8 9.**

36 pt

The quick brown fox jumps over the lazy dog. 0 1 2 3 4 5 6 7 8 9. *The fox jumps over the lazy dog. 0 1 2 3 4 5 6 7 8 9.* **The fox jumps over the lazy dog. 0 1**

Black: 75% Tint
HEX #636466

6 pt
The quick brown fox jumps over the lazy dog. 0 1 2 3 4 5 6 7 8 9.
The quick brown fox jumps over the lazy dog. 0 1 2 3 4 5 6 7 8 9.
The quick brown fox jumps over the lazy dog. 0 1 2 3 4 5 6 7 8 9.

7 pt
The quick brown fox jumps over the lazy dog. 0 1 2 3 4 5 6 7 8 9. *The quick brown fox jumps over the lazy dog. 0 1 2 3 4 5 6 7 8 9.* **The quick brown fox jumps over the lazy dog. 0 1 2 3 4 5 6 7 8 9.**

8 pt
The quick brown fox jumps over the lazy dog. 0 1 2 3 4 5 6 7 8 9. *The quick brown fox jumps over the lazy dog. 0 1 2 3 4 5 6 7 8 9.* **The quick brown fox jumps over the lazy dog. 0 1 2 3 4 5 6 7 8 9.**

9 pt
The quick brown fox jumps over the lazy dog. 0 1 2 3 4 5 6 7 8 9. *The quick brown fox jumps over the lazy dog. 0 1 2 3 4 5 6 7 8 9.* **The quick brown fox jumps over the lazy dog. 0 1 2 3 4 5 6 7 8 9.**

10 pt
The quick brown fox jumps over the lazy dog. 0 1 2 3 4 5 6 7 8 9. *The quick brown fox jumps over the lazy dog. 0 1 2 3 4 5 6 7 8 9.* **The quick brown fox jumps over the lazy dog. 0 1 2 3 4 5 6 7 8 9.**

12 pt
The quick brown fox jumps over the lazy dog. 0 1 2 3 4 5 6 7 8 9. *The quick brown fox jumps over the lazy dog. 0 1 2 3 4 5 6 7 8 9.* **The quick brown fox jumps over the lazy dog. 0 1 2 3 4 5 6 7 8 9.**

14 pt
The quick brown fox jumps over the lazy dog. 0 1 2 3 4 5 6 7 8 9. *The quick brown fox jumps over the lazy dog. 0 1 2 3 4 5 6 7 8 9.* **The quick**

Black: 50% Tint
HEX #939598

6 pt
The quick brown fox jumps over the lazy dog. 0 1 2 3 4 5 6 7 8 9.
The quick brown fox jumps over the lazy dog. 0 1 2 3 4 5 6 7 8 9.
The quick brown fox jumps over the lazy dog. 0 1 2 3 4 5 6 7 8 9.

7 pt
The quick brown fox jumps over the lazy dog. 0 1 2 3 4 5 6 7 8 9. *The quick brown fox jumps over the lazy dog. 0 1 2 3 4 5 6 7 8 9.* **The quick brown fox jumps over the lazy dog. 0 1 2 3 4 5 6 7 8 9.**

8 pt
The quick brown fox jumps over the lazy dog. 0 1 2 3 4 5 6 7 8 9. *The quick brown fox jumps over the lazy dog. 0 1 2 3 4 5 6 7 8 9.* **The quick brown fox jumps over the lazy dog. 0 1 2 3 4 5 6 7 8 9.**

9 pt
The quick brown fox jumps over the lazy dog. 0 1 2 3 4 5 6 7 8 9. *The quick brown fox jumps over the lazy dog. 0 1 2 3 4 5 6 7 8 9.* **The quick brown fox jumps over the lazy dog. 0 1 2 3 4 5 6 7 8 9.**

10 pt
The quick brown fox jumps over the lazy dog. 0 1 2 3 4 5 6 7 8 9. *The quick brown fox jumps over the lazy dog. 0 1 2 3 4 5 6 7 8 9.* **The quick brown fox jumps over the lazy dog. 0 1 2 3 4 5 6 7 8 9.**

12 pt
The quick brown fox jumps over the lazy dog. 0 1 2 3 4 5 6 7 8 9. *The quick brown fox jumps over the lazy dog. 0 1 2 3 4 5 6 7 8 9.* **The quick brown fox jumps over the lazy dog. 0 1 2 3 4 5 6 7 8 9.**

14 pt
The quick brown fox jumps over the lazy dog. 0 1 2 3 4 5 6 7 8 9. *The quick brown fox jumps over the lazy dog. 0 1 2 3 4 5 6 7 8 9.* **The quick**

Black: 25% Tint
HEX #C7C8CA

6 pt
The quick brown fox jumps over the lazy dog. 0 1 2 3 4 5 6 7 8 9.
The quick brown fox jumps over the lazy dog. 0 1 2 3 4 5 6 7 8 9.
The quick brown fox jumps over the lazy dog. 0 1 2 3 4 5 6 7 8 9.

7 pt
The quick brown fox jumps over the lazy dog. 0 1 2 3 4 5 6 7 8 9. *The quick brown fox jumps over the lazy dog. 0 1 2 3 4 5 6 7 8 9.* **The quick brown fox jumps over the lazy dog. 0 1 2 3 4 5 6 7 8 9.**

8 pt
The quick brown fox jumps over the lazy dog. 0 1 2 3 4 5 6 7 8 9. *The quick brown fox jumps over the lazy dog. 0 1 2 3 4 5 6 7 8 9.* **The quick brown fox jumps over the lazy dog. 0 1 2 3 4 5 6 7 8 9.**

9 pt
The quick brown fox jumps over the lazy dog. 0 1 2 3 4 5 6 7 8 9. *The quick brown fox jumps over the lazy dog. 0 1 2 3 4 5 6 7 8 9.* **The quick brown fox jumps over the lazy dog. 0 1 2 3 4 5 6 7 8 9.**

10 pt
The quick brown fox jumps over the lazy dog. 0 1 2 3 4 5 6 7 8 9. *The quick brown fox jumps over the lazy dog. 0 1 2 3 4 5 6 7 8 9.* **The quick brown fox jumps over the lazy dog. 0 1 2 3 4 5 6 7 8 9.**

12 pt
The quick brown fox jumps over the lazy dog. 0 1 2 3 4 5 6 7 8 9. *The quick brown fox jumps over the lazy dog. 0 1 2 3 4 5 6 7 8 9.* **The quick brown fox jumps over the lazy dog. 0 1 2 3 4 5 6 7 8 9.**

14 pt
The quick brown fox jumps over the lazy dog. 0 1 2 3 4 5 6 7 8 9. *The quick brown fox jumps over the lazy dog. 0 1 2 3 4 5 6 7 8 9.* **The quick**

Black: 10% Tint
HEX #E6E7E8

6 pt
The quick brown fox jumps over the lazy dog. 0 1 2 3 4 5 6 7 8 9.
The quick brown fox jumps over the lazy dog. 0 1 2 3 4 5 6 7 8 9.
The quick brown fox jumps over the lazy dog. 0 1 2 3 4 5 6 7 8 9.

7 pt
The quick brown fox jumps over the lazy dog. 0 1 2 3 4 5 6 7 8 9. *The quick brown fox jumps over the lazy dog. 0 1 2 3 4 5 6 7 8 9.* **The quick brown fox jumps over the lazy dog. 0 1 2 3 4 5 6 7 8 9.**

8 pt
The quick brown fox jumps over the lazy dog. 0 1 2 3 4 5 6 7 8 9. *The quick brown fox jumps over the lazy dog. 0 1 2 3 4 5 6 7 8 9.* **The quick brown fox jumps over the lazy dog. 0 1 2 3 4 5 6 7 8 9.**

9 pt
The quick brown fox jumps over the lazy dog. 0 1 2 3 4 5 6 7 8 9. *The quick brown fox jumps over the lazy dog. 0 1 2 3 4 5 6 7 8 9.* **The quick brown fox jumps over the lazy dog. 0 1 2 3 4 5 6 7 8 9.**

10 pt
The quick brown fox jumps over the lazy dog. 0 1 2 3 4 5 6 7 8 9. *The quick brown fox jumps over the lazy dog. 0 1 2 3 4 5 6 7 8 9.* **The quick brown fox jumps over the lazy dog. 0 1 2 3 4 5 6 7 8 9.**

12 pt
The quick brown fox jumps over the lazy dog. 0 1 2 3 4 5 6 7 8 9. *The quick brown fox jumps over the lazy dog. 0 1 2 3 4 5 6 7 8 9.* **The quick brown fox jumps over the lazy dog. 0 1 2 3 4 5 6 7 8 9.**

14 pt
The quick brown fox jumps over the lazy dog. 0 1 2 3 4 5 6 7 8 9. *The quick brown fox jumps over the lazy dog. 0 1 2 3 4 5 6 7 8 9.* **The quick**

AVENIR NEXT

4 pt
The quick brown fox jumps over the lazy dog. 0 1 2 3 4 5 6 7 8 9. *The quick brown fox jumps over the lazy dog. 0 1 2 3 4 5 6 7 8 9.* **The quick brown fox jumps over the lazy dog. 0 1 2 3 4 5 6 7 8 9.**

5 pt
The quick brown fox jumps over the lazy dog. 0 1 2 3 4 5 6 7 8 9. *The quick brown fox jumps over the lazy dog. 0 1 2 3 4 5 6 7 8 9.* **The quick brown fox jumps over the lazy dog. 0 1 2 3 4 5 6 7 8 9.**

6 pt
The quick brown fox jumps over the lazy dog. 0 1 2 3 4 5 6 7 8 9. *The quick brown fox jumps over the lazy dog. 0 1 2 3 4 5 6 7 8 9.* **The quick brown fox jumps over the lazy dog. 0 1 2 3 4 5 6 7 8 9.**

7 pt
The quick brown fox jumps over the lazy dog. 0 1 2 3 4 5 6 7 8 9. *The quick brown fox jumps over the lazy dog. 0 1 2 3 4 5 6 7 8 9.* **The quick brown fox jumps over the lazy dog. 0 1 2 3 4 5 6 7 8 9.**

8 pt
The quick brown fox jumps over the lazy dog. 0 1 2 3 4 5 6 7 8 9. *The quick brown fox jumps over the lazy dog. 0 1 2 3 4 5 6 7 8 9.* **The quick brown fox jumps over the lazy dog. 0 1 2 3 4 5 6 7 8 9.**

9 pt
The quick brown fox jumps over the lazy dog. 0 1 2 3 4 5 6 7 8 9. *The quick brown fox jumps over the lazy dog. 0 1 2 3 4 5 6 7 8 9.* **The quick brown fox jumps over the lazy dog. 0 1 2 3 4 5 6 7 8 9.**

10 pt
The quick brown fox jumps over the lazy dog. 0 1 2 3 4 5 6 7 8 9. *The quick brown fox jumps over the lazy dog. 0 1 2 3 4 5 6 7 8 9.* **The quick brown fox jumps over the lazy dog. 0 1 2 3 4 5 6 7 8 9.**

12 pt
The quick brown fox jumps over the lazy dog. 0 1 2 3 4 5 6 7 8 9. *The quick brown fox jumps over the lazy dog. 0 1 2 3 4 5 6 7 8 9.* **The quick brown fox jumps over the lazy dog. 0 1 2 3 4 5 6 7 8 9.**

14 pt
The quick brown fox jumps over the lazy dog. 0 1 2 3 4 5 6 7 8 9. *The quick brown fox jumps over the lazy dog. 0 1 2 3 4 5 6 7 8 9.* **The quick brown fox jumps over the lazy dog. 0 1 2 3 4 5 6 7 8 9.**

16 pt
The quick brown fox jumps over the lazy dog. 0 1 2 3 4 5 6 7 8 9. *The quick brown fox jumps over the lazy dog. 0 1 2 3 4 5 6 7 8 9.* **The quick brown fox jumps over the lazy dog. 0 1 2 3 4 5 6 7 8 9.**

18 pt

The quick brown fox jumps over the lazy dog. 0 1 2 3 4 5 6 7 8 9. *The quick brown fox jumps over the lazy dog. 0 1 2 3 4 5 6 7 8 9.* **The quick brown fox jumps over the lazy dog. 0 1 2 3 4 5 6 7 8 9.**

24 pt

The quick brown fox jumps over the lazy dog. 0 1 2 3 4 5 6 7 8 9. *The quick brown fox jumps over the lazy dog. 0 1 2 3 4 5 6 7 8 9.* **The quick brown fox jumps over the lazy dog. 0 1 2 3 4 5 6 7 8 9.**

36 pt

The quick brown fox jumps over the lazy dog. 0 1 2 3 4 5 6 7 8 9. *The quick brown fox jumps over the lazy dog. 0 1 2 3 4 5 6 7 8 9.* **The quick brown**

Black: 75% Tint
HEX #636466

6 pt

The quick brown fox jumps over the lazy dog. 0 1 2 3 4 5 6 7 8 9.
The quick brown fox jumps over the lazy dog. 0 1 2 3 4 5 6 7 8 9.
The quick brown fox jumps over the lazy dog. 0 1 2 3 4 5 6 7 8 9.

7 pt

The quick brown fox jumps over the lazy dog. 0 1 2 3 4 5 6 7 8 9. *The quick brown fox jumps over the lazy dog. 0 1 2 3 4 5 6 7 8 9.* **The quick brown fox jumps over the lazy dog. 0 1 2 3 4 5 6 7 8 9.**

8 pt

The quick brown fox jumps over the lazy dog. 0 1 2 3 4 5 6 7 8 9. *The quick brown fox jumps over the lazy dog. 0 1 2 3 4 5 6 7 8 9.* **The quick brown fox jumps over the lazy dog. 0 1 2 3 4 5 6 7 8 9.**

9 pt

The quick brown fox jumps over the lazy dog. 0 1 2 3 4 5 6 7 8 9. *The quick brown fox jumps over the lazy dog. 0 1 2 3 4 5 6 7 8 9.* **The quick brown fox jumps over the lazy dog. 0 1 2 3 4 5 6 7 8 9.**

10 pt

The quick brown fox jumps over the lazy dog. 0 1 2 3 4 5 6 7 8 9. *The quick brown fox jumps over the lazy dog. 0 1 2 3 4 5 6 7 8 9.* **The quick brown fox jumps over the lazy dog. 0 1 2 3 4 5 6 7 8 9.**

12 pt

The quick brown fox jumps over the lazy dog. 0 1 2 3 4 5 6 7 8 9. *The quick brown fox jumps over the lazy dog. 0 1 2 3 4 5 6 7 8 9.* **The quick brown fox jumps over the lazy dog. 0 1 2 3 4 5 6 7 8 9.**

14 pt

The quick brown fox jumps over the lazy dog. 0 1 2 3 4 5 6 7 8 9. *The quick brown fox jumps over the lazy dog.*

Black: 50% Tint
HEX #939598

6 pt

The quick brown fox jumps over the lazy dog. 0 1 2 3 4 5 6 7 8 9.
The quick brown fox jumps over the lazy dog. 0 1 2 3 4 5 6 7 8 9.
The quick brown fox jumps over the lazy dog. 0 1 2 3 4 5 6 7 8 9.

7 pt

The quick brown fox jumps over the lazy dog. 0 1 2 3 4 5 6 7 8 9. *The quick brown fox jumps over the lazy dog. 0 1 2 3 4 5 6 7 8 9.* **The quick brown fox jumps over the lazy dog. 0 1 2 3 4 5 6 7 8 9.**

8 pt

The quick brown fox jumps over the lazy dog. 0 1 2 3 4 5 6 7 8 9. *The quick brown fox jumps over the lazy dog. 0 1 2 3 4 5 6 7 8 9.* **The quick brown fox jumps over the lazy dog. 0 1 2 3 4 5 6 7 8 9.**

9 pt

The quick brown fox jumps over the lazy dog. 0 1 2 3 4 5 6 7 8 9. *The quick brown fox jumps over the lazy dog. 0 1 2 3 4 5 6 7 8 9.* **The quick brown fox jumps over the lazy dog. 0 1 2 3 4 5 6 7 8 9.**

10 pt

The quick brown fox jumps over the lazy dog. 0 1 2 3 4 5 6 7 8 9. *The quick brown fox jumps over the lazy dog. 0 1 2 3 4 5 6 7 8 9.* **The quick brown fox jumps over the lazy dog. 0 1 2 3 4 5 6 7 8 9.**

12 pt

The quick brown fox jumps over the lazy dog. 0 1 2 3 4 5 6 7 8 9. *The quick brown fox jumps over the lazy dog. 0 1 2 3 4 5 6 7 8 9.* **The quick brown fox jumps over the lazy dog. 0 1 2 3 4 5 6 7 8 9.**

14 pt

The quick brown fox jumps over the lazy dog. 0 1 2 3 4 5 6 7 8 9. *The quick brown fox jumps over the lazy dog.*

Black: 25% Tint
HEX #C7C8CA

6 pt
The quick brown fox jumps over the lazy dog. 0 1 2 3 4 5 6 7 8 9.
The quick brown fox jumps over the lazy dog. 0 1 2 3 4 5 6 7 8 9.
The quick brown fox jumps over the lazy dog. 0 1 2 3 4 5 6 7 8 9.

7 pt
The quick brown fox jumps over the lazy dog. 0 1 2 3 4 5 6 7 8 9. *The quick brown fox jumps over the lazy dog. 0 1 2 3 4 5 6 7 8 9.* **The quick brown fox jumps over the lazy dog. 0 1 2 3 4 5 6 7 8 9.**

8 pt
The quick brown fox jumps over the lazy dog. 0 1 2 3 4 5 6 7 8 9. *The quick brown fox jumps over the lazy dog. 0 1 2 3 4 5 6 7 8 9.* **The quick brown fox jumps over the lazy dog. 0 1 2 3 4 5 6 7 8 9.**

9 pt
The quick brown fox jumps over the lazy dog. 0 1 2 3 4 5 6 7 8 9. *The quick brown fox jumps over the lazy dog. 0 1 2 3 4 5 6 7 8 9.* **The quick brown fox jumps over the lazy dog. 0 1 2 3 4 5 6 7 8 9.**

10 pt
The quick brown fox jumps over the lazy dog. 0 1 2 3 4 5 6 7 8 9. *The quick brown fox jumps over the lazy dog. 0 1 2 3 4 5 6 7 8 9.* **The quick brown fox jumps over the lazy dog. 0 1 2 3 4 5 6 7 8 9.**

12 pt
The quick brown fox jumps over the lazy dog. 0 1 2 3 4 5 6 7 8 9. *The quick brown fox jumps over the lazy dog. 0 1 2 3 4 5 6 7 8 9.* **The quick brown fox jumps over the lazy dog. 0 1 2 3 4 5 6 7 8 9.**

14 pt
The quick brown fox jumps over the lazy dog. 0 1 2 3 4 5 6 7 8 9. *The quick brown fox jumps over the lazy dog.*

Black: 10% Tint
HEX #E6E7E8

6 pt
The quick brown fox jumps over the lazy dog. 0 1 2 3 4 5 6 7 8 9.
The quick brown fox jumps over the lazy dog. 0 1 2 3 4 5 6 7 8 9.
The quick brown fox jumps over the lazy dog. 0 1 2 3 4 5 6 7 8 9.

7 pt
The quick brown fox jumps over the lazy dog. 0 1 2 3 4 5 6 7 8 9. *The quick brown fox jumps over the lazy dog. 0 1 2 3 4 5 6 7 8 9.* **The quick brown fox jumps over the lazy dog. 0 1 2 3 4 5 6 7 8 9.**

8 pt
The quick brown fox jumps over the lazy dog. 0 1 2 3 4 5 6 7 8 9. *The quick brown fox jumps over the lazy dog. 0 1 2 3 4 5 6 7 8 9.* **The quick brown fox jumps over the lazy dog. 0 1 2 3 4 5 6 7 8 9.**

9 pt
The quick brown fox jumps over the lazy dog. 0 1 2 3 4 5 6 7 8 9. *The quick brown fox jumps over the lazy dog. 0 1 2 3 4 5 6 7 8 9.* **The quick brown fox jumps over the lazy dog. 0 1 2 3 4 5 6 7 8 9.**

10 pt
The quick brown fox jumps over the lazy dog. 0 1 2 3 4 5 6 7 8 9. *The quick brown fox jumps over the lazy dog. 0 1 2 3 4 5 6 7 8 9.* **The quick brown fox jumps over the lazy dog. 0 1 2 3 4 5 6 7 8 9.**

12 pt
The quick brown fox jumps over the lazy dog. 0 1 2 3 4 5 6 7 8 9. *The quick brown fox jumps over the lazy dog. 0 1 2 3 4 5 6 7 8 9.* **The quick brown fox jumps over the lazy dog. 0 1 2 3 4 5 6 7 8 9.**

14 pt
The quick brown fox jumps over the lazy dog. 0 1 2 3 4 5 6 7 8 9. *The quick brown fox jumps over the lazy dog.*

BRANDON GROTESQUE

4 pt
The quick brown fox jumps over the lazy dog. 0 1 2 3 4 5 6 7 8 9. *The quick brown fox jumps over the lazy dog. 0 1 2 3 4 5 6 7 8 9.* **The quick brown fox jumps over the lazy dog. 0 1 2 3 4 5 6 7 8 9.**

5 pt
The quick brown fox jumps over the lazy dog. 0 1 2 3 4 5 6 7 8 9. *The quick brown fox jumps over the lazy dog. 0 1 2 3 4 5 6 7 8 9.* **The quick brown fox jumps over the lazy dog. 0 1 2 3 4 5 6 7 8 9.**

6 pt
The quick brown fox jumps over the lazy dog. 0 1 2 3 4 5 6 7 8 9. *The quick brown fox jumps over the lazy dog. 0 1 2 3 4 5 6 7 8 9.* **The quick brown fox jumps over the lazy dog. 0 1 2 3 4 5 6 7 8 9.**

7 pt
The quick brown fox jumps over the lazy dog. 0 1 2 3 4 5 6 7 8 9. *The quick brown fox jumps over the lazy dog. 0 1 2 3 4 5 6 7 8 9.* **The quick brown fox jumps over the lazy dog. 0 1 2 3 4 5 6 7 8 9.**

8 pt
The quick brown fox jumps over the lazy dog. 0 1 2 3 4 5 6 7 8 9. *The quick brown fox jumps over the lazy dog. 0 1 2 3 4 5 6 7 8 9.* **The quick brown fox jumps over the lazy dog. 0 1 2 3 4 5 6 7 8 9.**

9 pt
The quick brown fox jumps over the lazy dog. 0 1 2 3 4 5 6 7 8 9. *The quick brown fox jumps over the lazy dog. 0 1 2 3 4 5 6 7 8 9.* **The quick brown fox jumps over the lazy dog. 0 1 2 3 4 5 6 7 8 9.**

10 pt
The quick brown fox jumps over the lazy dog. 0 1 2 3 4 5 6 7 8 9. *The quick brown fox jumps over the lazy dog. 0 1 2 3 4 5 6 7 8 9.* **The quick brown fox jumps over the lazy dog. 0 1 2 3 4 5 6 7 8 9.**

12 pt
The quick brown fox jumps over the lazy dog. 0 1 2 3 4 5 6 7 8 9. *The quick brown fox jumps over the lazy dog. 0 1 2 3 4 5 6 7 8 9.* **The quick brown fox jumps over the lazy dog. 0 1 2 3 4 5 6 7 8 9.**

14 pt
The quick brown fox jumps over the lazy dog. 0 1 2 3 4 5 6 7 8 9. *The quick brown fox jumps over the lazy dog. 0 1 2 3 4 5 6 7 8 9.* **The quick brown fox jumps over the lazy dog. 0 1 2 3 4 5 6 7 8 9.**

16 pt
The quick brown fox jumps over the lazy dog. 0 1 2 3 4 5 6 7 8 9. *The quick brown fox jumps over the lazy dog. 0 1 2 3 4 5 6 7 8 9.* **The quick brown fox jumps over the lazy dog. 0 1 2 3 4 5 6 7 8 9.**

18 pt
The quick brown fox jumps over the lazy dog. 0 1 2 3 4 5 6 7 8 9. *The quick brown fox jumps over the lazy dog. 0*

1 2 3 4 5 6 7 8 9. **The quick brown fox jumps over the lazy dog. 0 1 2 3 4 5 6 7 8 9.**

24 pt

The quick brown fox jumps over the lazy dog. 0 1 2 3 4 5 6 7 8 9. *The quick brown fox jumps over the lazy dog. 0 1 2 3 4 5 6 7 8 9.* **The quick brown fox jumps over the lazy dog. 0 1 2 3 4 5 6 7 8 9.**

36 pt

The quick brown fox jumps over the lazy dog. 0 1 2 3 4 5 6 7 8 9. *The quick brown fox jumps over the lazy dog. 0 1 2 3 4 5 6 7 8 9.* **The quick brown fox jumps over the lazy dog. 0 1 2 3 4 5 6 7 8 9.**

Black: 75% Tint
HEX #636466

6 pt
The quick brown fox jumps over the lazy dog. 0 1 2 3 4 5 6 7 8 9. *The quick brown fox jumps over the lazy dog. 0 1 2 3 4 5 6 7 8 9.* **The quick brown fox jumps over the lazy dog. 0 1 2 3 4 5 6 7 8 9.**

7 pt
The quick brown fox jumps over the lazy dog. 0 1 2 3 4 5 6 7 8 9. *The quick brown fox jumps over the lazy dog. 0 1 2 3 4 5 6 7 8 9.* **The quick brown fox jumps over the lazy dog. 0 1 2 3 4 5 6 7 8 9.**

8 pt
The quick brown fox jumps over the lazy dog. 0 1 2 3 4 5 6 7 8 9. *The quick brown fox jumps over the lazy dog. 0 1 2 3 4 5 6 7 8 9.* **The quick brown fox jumps over the lazy dog. 0 1 2 3 4 5 6 7 8 9.**

9 pt
The quick brown fox jumps over the lazy dog. 0 1 2 3 4 5 6 7 8 9. *The quick brown fox jumps over the lazy dog. 0 1 2 3 4 5 6 7 8 9.* **The quick brown fox jumps over the lazy dog. 0 1 2 3 4 5 6 7 8 9.**

10 pt
The quick brown fox jumps over the lazy dog. 0 1 2 3 4 5 6 7 8 9. *The quick brown fox jumps over the lazy dog. 0 1 2 3 4 5 6 7 8 9.* **The quick brown fox jumps over the lazy dog. 0 1 2 3 4 5 6 7 8 9.**

12 pt
The quick brown fox jumps over the lazy dog. 0 1 2 3 4 5 6 7 8 9. *The quick brown fox jumps over the lazy dog. 0 1 2 3 4 5 6 7 8 9.* **The quick brown fox jumps over the lazy dog. 0 1 2 3 4 5 6 7 8 9.**

14 pt
The quick brown fox jumps over the lazy dog. 0 1 2 3 4 5 6 7 8 9. *The quick brown fox jumps over the lazy dog. 0 1 2 3 4 5 6 7 8 9.* **The quick brown fox jumps over the lazy dog. 0 1 2 3 4 5 6 7 8 9.**

Black: 50% Tint
HEX #939598

6 pt
The quick brown fox jumps over the lazy dog. 0 1 2 3 4 5 6 7 8 9. *The quick brown fox jumps over the lazy dog. 0 1 2 3 4 5 6 7 8 9.* **The quick brown fox jumps over the lazy dog. 0 1 2 3 4 5 6 7 8 9.**

7 pt
The quick brown fox jumps over the lazy dog. 0 1 2 3 4 5 6 7 8 9. *The quick brown fox jumps over the lazy dog. 0 1 2 3 4 5 6 7 8 9.* **The quick brown fox jumps over the lazy dog. 0 1 2 3 4 5 6 7 8 9.**

8 pt
The quick brown fox jumps over the lazy dog. 0 1 2 3 4 5 6 7 8 9. *The quick brown fox jumps over the lazy dog. 0 1 2 3 4 5 6 7 8 9.* **The quick brown fox jumps over the lazy dog. 0 1 2 3 4 5 6 7 8 9.**

9 pt
The quick brown fox jumps over the lazy dog. 0 1 2 3 4 5 6 7 8 9. *The quick brown fox jumps over the lazy dog. 0 1 2 3 4 5 6 7 8 9.* **The quick brown fox jumps over the lazy dog. 0 1 2 3 4 5 6 7 8 9.**

10 pt
The quick brown fox jumps over the lazy dog. 0 1 2 3 4 5 6 7 8 9. *The quick brown fox jumps over the lazy dog. 0 1 2 3 4 5 6 7 8 9.* **The quick brown fox jumps over the lazy dog. 0 1 2 3 4 5 6 7 8 9.**

12 pt
The quick brown fox jumps over the lazy dog. 0 1 2 3 4 5 6 7 8 9. *The quick brown fox jumps over the lazy dog. 0 1 2 3 4 5 6 7 8 9.* **The quick brown fox jumps over the lazy dog. 0 1 2 3 4 5 6 7 8 9.**

14 pt
The quick brown fox jumps over the lazy dog. 0 1 2 3 4 5 6 7 8 9. *The quick brown fox jumps over the lazy dog. 0 1 2 3 4 5 6 7 8 9.* **The quick brown fox jumps over the lazy dog. 0 1 2 3 4 5 6 7 8 9.**

Black: 25% Tint
HEX #C7C8CA

6 pt
The quick brown fox jumps over the lazy dog. 0 1 2 3 4 5 6 7 8 9. The quick brown fox jumps over the lazy dog. 0 1 2 3 4 5 6 7 8 9. The quick brown fox jumps over the lazy dog. 0 1 2 3 4 5 6 7 8 9.

7 pt
The quick brown fox jumps over the lazy dog. 0 1 2 3 4 5 6 7 8 9. The quick brown fox jumps over the lazy dog. 0 1 2 3 4 5 6 7 8 9. The quick brown fox jumps over the lazy dog. 0 1 2 3 4 5 6 7 8 9.

8 pt
The quick brown fox jumps over the lazy dog. 0 1 2 3 4 5 6 7 8 9. The quick brown fox jumps over the lazy dog. 0 1 2 3 4 5 6 7 8 9. The quick brown fox jumps over the lazy dog. 0 1 2 3 4 5 6 7 8 9.

9 pt
The quick brown fox jumps over the lazy dog. 0 1 2 3 4 5 6 7 8 9. The quick brown fox jumps over the lazy dog. 0 1 2 3 4 5 6 7 8 9. **The quick brown fox jumps over the lazy dog. 0 1 2 3 4 5 6 7 8 9.**

10 pt
The quick brown fox jumps over the lazy dog. 0 1 2 3 4 5 6 7 8 9. *The quick brown fox jumps over the lazy dog. 0 1 2 3 4 5 6 7 8 9.* **The quick brown fox jumps over the lazy dog. 0 1 2 3 4 5 6 7 8 9.**

12 pt
The quick brown fox jumps over the lazy dog. 0 1 2 3 4 5 6 7 8 9. *The quick brown fox jumps over the lazy dog. 0 1 2 3 4 5 6 7 8 9.* **The quick brown fox jumps over the lazy dog. 0 1 2 3 4 5 6 7 8 9.**

14 pt
The quick brown fox jumps over the lazy dog. 0 1 2 3 4 5 6 7 8 9. *The quick brown fox jumps over the lazy dog. 0 1 2 3 4 5 6 7 8 9.* **The quick brown fox jumps over the lazy dog. 0 1 2 3 4 5 6 7 8 9.**

Black: 10% Tint
HEX #E6E7E8

6 pt
The quick brown fox jumps over the lazy dog. 0 1 2 3 4 5 6 7 8 9. The quick brown fox jumps over the lazy dog. 0 1 2 3 4 5 6 7 8 9. The quick brown fox jumps over the lazy dog. 0 1 2 3 4 5 6 7 8 9.

7 pt
The quick brown fox jumps over the lazy dog. 0 1 2 3 4 5 6 7 8 9. The quick brown fox jumps over the lazy dog. 0 1 2 3 4 5 6 7 8 9. The quick brown fox jumps over the lazy dog. 0 1 2 3 4 5 6 7 8 9.

8 pt
The quick brown fox jumps over the lazy dog. 0 1 2 3 4 5 6 7 8 9. The quick brown fox jumps over the lazy dog. 0 1 2 3 4 5 6 7 8 9. The quick brown fox jumps over the lazy dog. 0 1 2 3 4 5 6 7 8 9.

9 pt
The quick brown fox jumps over the lazy dog. 0 1 2 3 4 5 6 7 8 9. The quick brown fox jumps over the lazy dog. 0 1 2 3 4 5 6 7 8 9. **The quick brown fox jumps over the lazy dog. 0 1 2 3 4 5 6 7 8 9.**

10 pt
The quick brown fox jumps over the lazy dog. 0 1 2 3 4 5 6 7 8 9. *The quick brown fox jumps over the lazy dog. 0 1 2 3 4 5 6 7 8 9.* **The quick brown fox jumps over the lazy dog. 0 1 2 3 4 5 6 7 8 9.**

12 pt
The quick brown fox jumps over the lazy dog. 0 1 2 3 4 5 6 7 8 9. *The quick brown fox jumps over the lazy dog. 0 1 2 3 4 5 6 7 8 9.* **The quick brown fox jumps over the lazy dog. 0 1 2 3 4 5 6 7 8 9.**

14 pt
The quick brown fox jumps over the lazy dog. 0 1 2 3 4 5 6 7 8 9. *The quick brown fox jumps over the lazy dog. 0 1 2 3 4 5 6 7 8 9.* **The quick brown fox jumps over the lazy dog. 0 1 2 3 4 5 6 7 8 9.**

FUTURA

4 pt
The quick brown fox jumps over the lazy dog. 0 1 2 3 4 5 6 7 8 9. The quick brown fox jumps over the lazy dog. 0 1 2 3 4 5 6 7 8 9. **The quick brown fox jumps over the lazy dog. 0 1 2 3 4 5 6 7 8 9.**

5 pt
The quick brown fox jumps over the lazy dog. 0 1 2 3 4 5 6 7 8 9. *The quick brown fox jumps over the lazy dog. 0 1 2 3 4 5 6 7 8 9.* **The quick brown fox jumps over the lazy dog. 0 1 2 3 4 5 6 7 8 9.**

6 pt
The quick brown fox jumps over the lazy dog. 0 1 2 3 4 5 6 7 8 9. *The quick brown fox jumps over the lazy dog. 0 1 2 3 4 5 6 7 8 9.* **The quick brown fox jumps over the lazy dog. 0 1 2 3 4 5 6 7 8 9.**

7 pt
The quick brown fox jumps over the lazy dog. 0 1 2 3 4 5 6 7 8 9. *The quick brown fox jumps over the lazy dog. 0 1 2 3 4 5 6 7 8 9.* **The quick brown fox jumps over the lazy dog. 0 1 2 3 4 5 6 7 8 9.**

8 pt
The quick brown fox jumps over the lazy dog. 0 1 2 3 4 5 6 7 8 9. *The quick brown fox jumps over the lazy dog. 0 1 2 3 4 5 6 7 8 9.* **The quick brown fox jumps over the lazy dog. 0 1 2 3 4 5 6 7 8 9.**

9 pt
The quick brown fox jumps over the lazy dog. 0 1 2 3 4 5 6 7 8 9. *The quick brown fox jumps over the lazy dog. 0 1 2 3 4 5 6 7 8 9.* **The quick brown fox jumps over the lazy dog. 0 1 2 3 4 5 6 7 8 9.**

10 pt
The quick brown fox jumps over the lazy dog. 0 1 2 3 4 5 6 7 8 9. *The quick brown fox jumps over the lazy dog. 0 1 2 3 4 5 6 7 8 9.* **The quick brown fox jumps over the lazy dog. 0 1 2 3 4 5 6 7 8 9.**

12 pt
The quick brown fox jumps over the lazy dog. 0 1 2 3 4 5 6 7 8 9. *The quick brown fox jumps over the lazy dog. 0 1 2 3 4 5 6 7 8 9.* **The quick brown fox jumps over the lazy dog. 0 1 2 3 4 5 6 7 8 9.**

14 pt
The quick brown fox jumps over the lazy dog. 0 1 2 3 4 5 6 7 8 9. *The quick brown fox jumps over the lazy dog. 0 1 2 3 4 5 6 7 8 9.* **The quick brown fox jumps over the lazy dog. 0 1 2 3 4 5 6 7 8 9.**

16 pt
The quick brown fox jumps over the lazy dog. 0 1 2 3 4 5 6 7 8 9. *The quick brown fox jumps over the lazy dog. 0 1 2 3 4 5 6 7 8 9.* **The quick brown**

fox jumps over the lazy dog. 0 1 2 3 4 5 6 7 8 9.

18 pt

The quick brown fox jumps over the lazy dog. 0 1 2 3 4 5 6 7 8 9. *The quick brown fox jumps over the lazy dog. 0 1 2 3 4 5 6 7 8 9.* **The quick brown fox jumps over the lazy dog. 0 1 2 3 4 5 6 7 8 9.**

24 pt

The quick brown fox jumps over the lazy dog. 0 1 2 3 4 5 6 7 8 9. *The quick brown fox jumps over the lazy dog. 0 1 2 3 4 5 6 7 8 9.* **The quick brown fox jumps over the lazy dog. 0 1 2 3 4 5 6 7 8 9.**

36 pt

The quick brown fox jumps over the lazy dog. 0 1 2 3 4 5 6 7 8 9. *The quick brown fox jumps over the lazy*

Black: 75% Tint
HEX #636466

6 pt
The quick brown fox jumps over the lazy dog. 0 1 2 3 4 5 6 7 8 9. *The quick brown fox jumps over the lazy dog. 0 1 2 3 4 5 6 7 8 9.* **The quick brown fox jumps over the lazy dog. 0 1 2 3 4 5 6 7 8 9.**

7 pt
The quick brown fox jumps over the lazy dog. 0 1 2 3 4 5 6 7 8 9. *The quick brown fox jumps over the lazy dog. 0 1 2 3 4 5 6 7 8 9.* **The quick brown fox jumps over the lazy dog. 0 1 2 3 4 5 6 7 8 9.**

8 pt
The quick brown fox jumps over the lazy dog. 0 1 2 3 4 5 6 7 8 9. *The quick brown fox jumps over the lazy dog. 0 1 2 3 4 5 6 7 8 9.* **The quick brown fox jumps over the lazy dog. 0 1 2 3 4 5 6 7 8 9.**

9 pt
The quick brown fox jumps over the lazy dog. 0 1 2 3 4 5 6 7 8 9. *The quick brown fox jumps over the lazy dog. 0 1 2 3 4 5 6 7 8 9.* **The quick brown fox jumps over the lazy dog. 0 1 2 3 4 5 6 7 8 9.**

10 pt
The quick brown fox jumps over the lazy dog. 0 1 2 3 4 5 6 7 8 9. *The quick brown fox jumps over the lazy dog. 0 1 2 3 4 5 6 7 8 9.* **The quick brown fox jumps over the lazy dog. 0 1 2 3 4 5 6 7 8 9.**

12 pt
The quick brown fox jumps over the lazy dog. 0 1 2 3 4 5 6 7 8 9. *The quick brown fox jumps over the lazy dog. 0 1 2 3 4 5 6 7 8 9.* **The quick brown fox jumps over the lazy dog. 0 1 2 3 4 5 6 7 8 9.**

14 pt
The quick brown fox jumps over the lazy dog. 0 1 2 3 4 5 6 7 8 9. *The quick brown*

Black: 50% Tint
HEX #939598

6 pt
The quick brown fox jumps over the lazy dog. 0 1 2 3 4 5 6 7 8 9. *The quick brown fox jumps over the lazy dog. 0 1 2 3 4 5 6 7 8 9.* **The quick brown fox jumps over the lazy dog. 0 1 2 3 4 5 6 7 8 9.**

7 pt
The quick brown fox jumps over the lazy dog. 0 1 2 3 4 5 6 7 8 9. *The quick brown fox jumps over the lazy dog. 0 1 2 3 4 5 6 7 8 9.* **The quick brown fox jumps over the lazy dog. 0 1 2 3 4 5 6 7 8 9.**

8 pt
The quick brown fox jumps over the lazy dog. 0 1 2 3 4 5 6 7 8 9. *The quick brown fox jumps over the lazy dog. 0 1 2 3 4 5 6 7 8 9.* **The quick brown fox jumps over the lazy dog. 0 1 2 3 4 5 6 7 8 9.**

9 pt
The quick brown fox jumps over the lazy dog. 0 1 2 3 4 5 6 7 8 9. *The quick brown fox jumps over the lazy dog. 0 1 2 3 4 5 6 7 8 9.* **The quick brown fox jumps over the lazy dog. 0 1 2 3 4 5 6 7 8 9.**

10 pt
The quick brown fox jumps over the lazy dog. 0 1 2 3 4 5 6 7 8 9. *The quick brown fox jumps over the lazy dog. 0 1 2 3 4 5 6 7 8 9.* **The quick brown fox jumps over the lazy dog. 0 1 2 3 4 5 6 7 8 9.**

12 pt
The quick brown fox jumps over the lazy dog. 0 1 2 3 4 5 6 7 8 9. *The quick brown fox jumps over the lazy dog. 0 1 2 3 4 5 6 7 8 9.* **The quick brown fox jumps over the lazy dog. 0 1 2 3 4 5 6 7 8 9.**

14 pt
The quick brown fox jumps over the lazy dog. 0 1 2 3 4 5 6 7 8 9. *The quick brown*

Black: 25% Tint
HEX #C7C8CA

6 pt
The quick brown fox jumps over the lazy dog. 0 1 2 3 4 5 6 7 8 9. *The quick brown fox jumps over the lazy dog. 0 1 2 3 4 5 6 7 8 9.* **The quick brown fox jumps over the lazy dog. 0 1 2 3 4 5 6 7 8 9.**

7 pt
The quick brown fox jumps over the lazy dog. 0 1 2 3 4 5 6 7 8 9. *The quick brown fox jumps over the lazy dog. 0 1 2 3 4 5 6 7 8 9.* **The quick brown fox jumps over the lazy dog. 0 1 2 3 4 5 6 7 8 9.**

8 pt
The quick brown fox jumps over the lazy dog. 0 1 2 3 4 5 6 7 8 9. *The quick brown fox jumps over the lazy dog. 0 1 2 3 4 5 6 7 8 9.* **The quick brown fox jumps over the lazy dog. 0 1 2 3 4 5 6 7 8 9.**

9 pt
The quick brown fox jumps over the lazy dog. 0 1 2 3 4 5 6 7 8 9. *The quick brown fox jumps over the lazy dog. 0 1 2 3 4 5 6 7 8 9.* **The quick brown fox jumps over the lazy dog. 0 1 2 3 4 5 6 7 8 9.**

10 pt
The quick brown fox jumps over the lazy dog. 0 1 2 3 4 5 6 7 8 9. *The quick brown fox jumps over the lazy dog. 0 1 2 3 4 5 6 7 8 9.* **The quick brown fox jumps over the lazy dog. 0 1 2 3 4 5 6 7 8 9.**

12 pt
The quick brown fox jumps over the lazy dog. 0 1 2 3 4 5 6 7 8 9. *The quick brown fox jumps over the lazy dog. 0 1 2 3 4 5 6 7 8 9.* **The quick brown fox jumps over the lazy dog. 0 1 2 3 4 5 6 7 8 9.**

14 pt
The quick brown fox jumps over the lazy dog. 0 1 2 3 4 5 6 7 8 9. *The quick brown*

Black: 10% Tint
HEX #E6E7E8

6 pt
The quick brown fox jumps over the lazy dog. 0 1 2 3 4 5 6 7 8 9. *The quick brown fox jumps over the lazy dog. 0 1 2 3 4 5 6 7 8 9.* **The quick brown fox jumps over the lazy dog. 0 1 2 3 4 5 6 7 8 9.**

7 pt
The quick brown fox jumps over the lazy dog. 0 1 2 3 4 5 6 7 8 9. *The quick brown fox jumps over the lazy dog. 0 1 2 3 4 5 6 7 8 9.* **The quick brown fox jumps over the lazy dog. 0 1 2 3 4 5 6 7 8 9.**

8 pt
The quick brown fox jumps over the lazy dog. 0 1 2 3 4 5 6 7 8 9. *The quick brown fox jumps over the lazy dog. 0 1 2 3 4 5 6 7 8 9.* **The quick brown fox jumps over the lazy dog. 0 1 2 3 4 5 6 7 8 9.**

9 pt
The quick brown fox jumps over the lazy dog. 0 1 2 3 4 5 6 7 8 9. *The quick brown fox jumps over the lazy dog. 0 1 2 3 4 5 6 7 8 9.* **The quick brown fox jumps over the lazy dog. 0 1 2 3 4 5 6 7 8 9.**

10 pt
The quick brown fox jumps over the lazy dog. 0 1 2 3 4 5 6 7 8 9. *The quick brown fox jumps over the lazy dog. 0 1 2 3 4 5 6 7 8 9.* **The quick brown fox jumps over the lazy dog. 0 1 2 3 4 5 6 7 8 9.**

12 pt
The quick brown fox jumps over the lazy dog. 0 1 2 3 4 5 6 7 8 9. *The quick brown fox jumps over the lazy dog. 0 1 2 3 4 5 6 7 8 9.* **The quick brown fox jumps over the lazy dog. 0 1 2 3 4 5 6 7 8 9.**

14 pt
The quick brown fox jumps over the lazy dog. 0 1 2 3 4 5 6 7 8 9. *The quick brown*

HELVETICA NEUE

4 pt
The quick brown fox jumps over the lazy dog. 0 1 2 3 4 5 6 7 8 9. *The quick brown fox jumps over the lazy dog. 0 1 2 3 4 5 6 7 8 9.* **The quick brown fox jumps over the lazy dog. 0 1 2 3 4 5 6 7 8 9.**

5 pt
The quick brown fox jumps over the lazy dog. 0 1 2 3 4 5 6 7 8 9. *The quick brown fox jumps over the lazy dog. 0 1 2 3 4 5 6 7 8 9.* **The quick brown fox jumps over the lazy dog. 0 1 2 3 4 5 6 7 8 9.**

6 pt
The quick brown fox jumps over the lazy dog. 0 1 2 3 4 5 6 7 8 9. *The quick brown fox jumps over the lazy dog. 0 1 2 3 4 5 6 7 8 9.* **The quick brown fox jumps over the lazy dog. 0 1 2 3 4 5 6 7 8 9.**

7 pt
The quick brown fox jumps over the lazy dog. 0 1 2 3 4 5 6 7 8 9. *The quick brown fox jumps over the lazy dog. 0 1 2 3 4 5 6 7 8 9.* **The quick brown fox jumps over the lazy dog. 0 1 2 3 4 5 6 7 8 9.**

8 pt
The quick brown fox jumps over the lazy dog. 0 1 2 3 4 5 6 7 8 9. *The quick brown fox jumps over the lazy dog. 0 1 2 3 4 5 6 7 8 9.* **The quick brown fox jumps over the lazy dog. 0 1 2 3 4 5 6 7 8 9.**

9 pt
The quick brown fox jumps over the lazy dog. 0 1 2 3 4 5 6 7 8 9. *The quick brown fox jumps over the lazy dog. 0 1 2 3 4 5 6 7 8 9.* **The quick brown fox jumps over the lazy dog. 0 1 2 3 4 5 6 7 8 9.**

10 pt
The quick brown fox jumps over the lazy dog. 0 1 2 3 4 5 6 7 8 9. *The quick brown fox jumps over the lazy dog. 0 1 2 3 4 5 6 7 8 9.* **The quick brown fox jumps over the lazy dog. 0 1 2 3 4 5 6 7 8 9.**

12 pt
The quick brown fox jumps over the lazy dog. 0 1 2 3 4 5 6 7 8 9. *The quick brown fox jumps over the lazy dog. 0 1 2 3 4 5 6 7 8 9.* **The quick brown fox jumps over the lazy dog. 0 1 2 3 4 5 6 7 8 9.**

14 pt
The quick brown fox jumps over the lazy dog. 0 1 2 3 4 5 6 7 8 9. *The quick brown fox jumps over the lazy dog. 0 1 2 3 4 5 6 7 8 9.* **The quick brown fox jumps over the lazy dog. 0 1 2 3 4 5 6 7 8 9.**

16 pt
The quick brown fox jumps over the lazy dog. 0 1 2 3 4 5 6 7 8 9. *The quick brown fox jumps over the lazy dog. 0 1 2 3 4 5 6 7 8 9.* **The quick brown fox jumps over the lazy dog. 0 1 2 3 4 5 6 7 8 9.**

18 pt

The quick brown fox jumps over the lazy dog. 0 1 2 3 4 5 6 7 8 9. *The quick brown fox jumps over the lazy dog. 0 1 2 3 4 5 6 7 8 9.* **The quick brown fox jumps over the lazy dog. 0 1 2 3 4 5 6 7 8 9.**

24 pt

The quick brown fox jumps over the lazy dog. 0 1 2 3 4 5 6 7 8 9. *The quick brown fox jumps over the lazy dog. 0 1 2 3 4 5 6 7 8 9.* **The quick brown fox jumps over the lazy dog. 0 1 2 3 4 5 6 7 8 9.**

36 pt

The quick brown fox jumps over the lazy dog. 0 1 2 3 4 5 6 7 8 9. *The quick brown fox jumps over the lazy dog. 0 1 2 3 4 5 6 7 8 9.* **The quick brown**

Black: 75% Tint
HEX #636466

6 pt
The quick brown fox jumps over the lazy dog. 0 1 2 3 4 5 6 7 8 9.
The quick brown fox jumps over the lazy dog. 0 1 2 3 4 5 6 7 8 9.
The quick brown fox jumps over the lazy dog. 0 1 2 3 4 5 6 7 8 9.

7 pt
The quick brown fox jumps over the lazy dog. 0 1 2 3 4 5 6 7 8 9. *The quick brown fox jumps over the lazy dog. 0 1 2 3 4 5 6 7 8 9.* **The quick brown fox jumps over the lazy dog. 0 1 2 3 4 5 6 7 8 9.**

8 pt
The quick brown fox jumps over the lazy dog. 0 1 2 3 4 5 6 7 8 9. *The quick brown fox jumps over the lazy dog. 0 1 2 3 4 5 6 7 8 9.* **The quick brown fox jumps over the lazy dog. 0 1 2 3 4 5 6 7 8 9.**

9 pt
The quick brown fox jumps over the lazy dog. 0 1 2 3 4 5 6 7 8 9. *The quick brown fox jumps over the lazy dog. 0 1 2 3 4 5 6 7 8 9.* **The quick brown fox jumps over the lazy dog. 0 1 2 3 4 5 6 7 8 9.**

10 pt
The quick brown fox jumps over the lazy dog. 0 1 2 3 4 5 6 7 8 9. *The quick brown fox jumps over the lazy dog. 0 1 2 3 4 5 6 7 8 9.* **The quick brown fox jumps over the lazy dog. 0 1 2 3 4 5 6 7 8 9.**

12 pt
The quick brown fox jumps over the lazy dog. 0 1 2 3 4 5 6 7 8 9. *The quick brown fox jumps over the lazy dog. 0 1 2 3 4 5 6 7 8 9.* **The quick brown fox jumps over the lazy dog. 0 1 2 3 4 5 6 7 8 9.**

14 pt
The quick brown fox jumps over the lazy dog. 0 1 2 3 4 5 6 7 8 9. *The quick brown fox jumps over the lazy dog. 0 1 2 3 4 5 6 7 8 9.* **The quick brown fox jumps over the**

Black: 50% Tint
HEX #939598

6 pt
The quick brown fox jumps over the lazy dog. 0 1 2 3 4 5 6 7 8 9.
The quick brown fox jumps over the lazy dog. 0 1 2 3 4 5 6 7 8 9.
The quick brown fox jumps over the lazy dog. 0 1 2 3 4 5 6 7 8 9.

7 pt
The quick brown fox jumps over the lazy dog. 0 1 2 3 4 5 6 7 8 9. *The quick brown fox jumps over the lazy dog. 0 1 2 3 4 5 6 7 8 9.* **The quick brown fox jumps over the lazy dog. 0 1 2 3 4 5 6 7 8 9.**

8 pt
The quick brown fox jumps over the lazy dog. 0 1 2 3 4 5 6 7 8 9. *The quick brown fox jumps over the lazy dog. 0 1 2 3 4 5 6 7 8 9.* **The quick brown fox jumps over the lazy dog. 0 1 2 3 4 5 6 7 8 9.**

9 pt
The quick brown fox jumps over the lazy dog. 0 1 2 3 4 5 6 7 8 9. *The quick brown fox jumps over the lazy dog. 0 1 2 3 4 5 6 7 8 9.* **The quick brown fox jumps over the lazy dog. 0 1 2 3 4 5 6 7 8 9.**

10 pt
The quick brown fox jumps over the lazy dog. 0 1 2 3 4 5 6 7 8 9. *The quick brown fox jumps over the lazy dog. 0 1 2 3 4 5 6 7 8 9.* **The quick brown fox jumps over the lazy dog. 0 1 2 3 4 5 6 7 8 9.**

12 pt
The quick brown fox jumps over the lazy dog. 0 1 2 3 4 5 6 7 8 9. *The quick brown fox jumps over the lazy dog. 0 1 2 3 4 5 6 7 8 9.* **The quick brown fox jumps over the lazy dog. 0 1 2 3 4 5 6 7 8 9.**

14 pt
The quick brown fox jumps over the lazy dog. 0 1 2 3 4 5 6 7 8 9. *The quick brown fox jumps over the lazy dog. 0 1 2 3 4 5 6 7 8 9.* **The quick brown fox jumps over the**

Black: 25% Tint
HEX #C7C8CA

6 pt
The quick brown fox jumps over the lazy dog. 0 1 2 3 4 5 6 7 8 9.
The quick brown fox jumps over the lazy dog. 0 1 2 3 4 5 6 7 8 9.
The quick brown fox jumps over the lazy dog. 0 1 2 3 4 5 6 7 8 9.

7 pt
The quick brown fox jumps over the lazy dog. 0 1 2 3 4 5 6 7 8 9. *The quick brown fox jumps over the lazy dog. 0 1 2 3 4 5 6 7 8 9.* **The quick brown fox jumps over the lazy dog. 0 1 2 3 4 5 6 7 8 9.**

8 pt
The quick brown fox jumps over the lazy dog. 0 1 2 3 4 5 6 7 8 9. *The quick brown fox jumps over the lazy dog. 0 1 2 3 4 5 6 7 8 9.* **The quick brown fox jumps over the lazy dog. 0 1 2 3 4 5 6 7 8 9.**

9 pt
The quick brown fox jumps over the lazy dog. 0 1 2 3 4 5 6 7 8 9. *The quick brown fox jumps over the lazy dog. 0 1 2 3 4 5 6 7 8 9.* **The quick brown fox jumps over the lazy dog. 0 1 2 3 4 5 6 7 8 9.**

10 pt
The quick brown fox jumps over the lazy dog. 0 1 2 3 4 5 6 7 8 9. *The quick brown fox jumps over the lazy dog. 0 1 2 3 4 5 6 7 8 9.* **The quick brown fox jumps over the lazy dog. 0 1 2 3 4 5 6 7 8 9.**

12 pt
The quick brown fox jumps over the lazy dog. 0 1 2 3 4 5 6 7 8 9. *The quick brown fox jumps over the lazy dog. 0 1 2 3 4 5 6 7 8 9.* **The quick brown fox jumps over the lazy dog. 0 1 2 3 4 5 6 7 8 9.**

14 pt
The quick brown fox jumps over the lazy dog. 0 1 2 3 4 5 6 7 8 9. *The quick brown fox jumps over the lazy dog. 0 1 2 3 4 5 6 7 8 9.* **The quick brown fox jumps over the**

Black: 10% Tint
HEX #E6E7E8

6 pt
The quick brown fox jumps over the lazy dog. 0 1 2 3 4 5 6 7 8 9.
The quick brown fox jumps over the lazy dog. 0 1 2 3 4 5 6 7 8 9.
The quick brown fox jumps over the lazy dog. 0 1 2 3 4 5 6 7 8 9.

7 pt
The quick brown fox jumps over the lazy dog. 0 1 2 3 4 5 6 7 8 9. *The quick brown fox jumps over the lazy dog. 0 1 2 3 4 5 6 7 8 9.* **The quick brown fox jumps over the lazy dog. 0 1 2 3 4 5 6 7 8 9.**

8 pt
The quick brown fox jumps over the lazy dog. 0 1 2 3 4 5 6 7 8 9. *The quick brown fox jumps over the lazy dog. 0 1 2 3 4 5 6 7 8 9.* **The quick brown fox jumps over the lazy dog. 0 1 2 3 4 5 6 7 8 9.**

9 pt
The quick brown fox jumps over the lazy dog. 0 1 2 3 4 5 6 7 8 9. *The quick brown fox jumps over the lazy dog. 0 1 2 3 4 5 6 7 8 9.* **The quick brown fox jumps over the lazy dog. 0 1 2 3 4 5 6 7 8 9.**

10 pt
The quick brown fox jumps over the lazy dog. 0 1 2 3 4 5 6 7 8 9. *The quick brown fox jumps over the lazy dog. 0 1 2 3 4 5 6 7 8 9.* **The quick brown fox jumps over the lazy dog. 0 1 2 3 4 5 6 7 8 9.**

12 pt
The quick brown fox jumps over the lazy dog. 0 1 2 3 4 5 6 7 8 9. *The quick brown fox jumps over the lazy dog. 0 1 2 3 4 5 6 7 8 9.* **The quick brown fox jumps over the lazy dog. 0 1 2 3 4 5 6 7 8 9.**

14 pt
The quick brown fox jumps over the lazy dog. 0 1 2 3 4 5 6 7 8 9. *The quick brown fox jumps over the lazy dog. 0 1 2 3 4 5 6 7 8 9.* **The quick brown fox jumps over the**

MYRIAD PRO

4 pt
The quick brown fox jumps over the lazy dog. 0 1 2 3 4 5 6 7 8 9. *The quick brown fox jumps over the lazy dog. 0 1 2 3 4 5 6 7 8 9.* **The quick brown fox jumps over the lazy dog. 0 1 2 3 4 5 6 7 8 9.**

5 pt
The quick brown fox jumps over the lazy dog. 0 1 2 3 4 5 6 7 8 9. *The quick brown fox jumps over the lazy dog. 0 1 2 3 4 5 6 7 8 9.* **The quick brown fox jumps over the lazy dog. 0 1 2 3 4 5 6 7 8 9.**

6 pt
The quick brown fox jumps over the lazy dog. 0 1 2 3 4 5 6 7 8 9. *The quick brown fox jumps over the lazy dog. 0 1 2 3 4 5 6 7 8 9.* **The quick brown fox jumps over the lazy dog. 0 1 2 3 4 5 6 7 8 9.**

7 pt
The quick brown fox jumps over the lazy dog. 0 1 2 3 4 5 6 7 8 9. *The quick brown fox jumps over the lazy dog. 0 1 2 3 4 5 6 7 8 9.* **The quick brown fox jumps over the lazy dog. 0 1 2 3 4 5 6 7 8 9.**

8 pt
The quick brown fox jumps over the lazy dog. 0 1 2 3 4 5 6 7 8 9. *The quick brown fox jumps over the lazy dog. 0 1 2 3 4 5 6 7 8 9.* **The quick brown fox jumps over the lazy dog. 0 1 2 3 4 5 6 7 8 9.**

9 pt
The quick brown fox jumps over the lazy dog. 0 1 2 3 4 5 6 7 8 9. *The quick brown fox jumps over the lazy dog. 0 1 2 3 4 5 6 7 8 9.* **The quick brown fox jumps over the lazy dog. 0 1 2 3 4 5 6 7 8 9.**

10 pt
The quick brown fox jumps over the lazy dog. 0 1 2 3 4 5 6 7 8 9. *The quick brown fox jumps over the lazy dog. 0 1 2 3 4 5 6 7 8 9.* **The quick brown fox jumps over the lazy dog. 0 1 2 3 4 5 6 7 8 9.**

12 pt
The quick brown fox jumps over the lazy dog. 0 1 2 3 4 5 6 7 8 9. *The quick brown fox jumps over the lazy dog. 0 1 2 3 4 5 6 7 8 9.* **The quick brown fox jumps over the lazy dog. 0 1 2 3 4 5 6 7 8 9.**

14 pt
The quick brown fox jumps over the lazy dog. 0 1 2 3 4 5 6 7 8 9. *The quick brown fox jumps over the lazy dog. 0 1 2 3 4 5 6 7 8 9.* **The quick brown fox jumps over the lazy dog. 0 1 2 3 4 5 6 7 8 9.**

16 pt
The quick brown fox jumps over the lazy dog. 0 1 2 3 4 5 6 7 8 9. *The quick brown fox jumps over the lazy dog. 0 1 2 3 4 5 6 7 8 9.* **The quick brown fox jumps over the lazy dog. 0 1 2 3 4 5 6 7 8 9.**

18 pt
The quick brown fox jumps over the lazy dog. 0 1 2

3 4 5 6 7 8 9. *The quick brown fox jumps over the lazy dog. 0 1 2 3 4 5 6 7 8 9.* **The quick brown fox jumps over the lazy dog. 0 1 2 3 4 5 6 7 8 9.**

24 pt

The quick brown fox jumps over the lazy dog. 0 1 2 3 4 5 6 7 8 9. *The quick brown fox jumps over the lazy dog. 0 1 2 3 4 5 6 7 8 9.* **The quick brown fox jumps over the lazy dog. 0 1 2 3 4 5 6 7 8 9.**

36 pt

The quick brown fox jumps over the lazy dog. 0 1 2 3 4 5 6 7 8 9. *The quick brown fox jumps over the lazy dog. 0 1 2 3 4 5 6 7 8 9.* **The quick brown fox jumps over the lazy dog. 0 1 2 3 4 5 6 7 8 9.**

Black: 75% Tint
HEX #636466

6 pt
The quick brown fox jumps over the lazy dog. 0 1 2 3 4 5 6 7 8 9. *The quick brown fox jumps over the lazy dog. 0 1 2 3 4 5 6 7 8 9.* **The quick brown fox jumps over the lazy dog. 0 1 2 3 4 5 6 7 8 9.**

7 pt
The quick brown fox jumps over the lazy dog. 0 1 2 3 4 5 6 7 8 9. *The quick brown fox jumps over the lazy dog. 0 1 2 3 4 5 6 7 8 9.* **The quick brown fox jumps over the lazy dog. 0 1 2 3 4 5 6 7 8 9.**

8 pt
The quick brown fox jumps over the lazy dog. 0 1 2 3 4 5 6 7 8 9. *The quick brown fox jumps over the lazy dog. 0 1 2 3 4 5 6 7 8 9.* **The quick brown fox jumps over the lazy dog. 0 1 2 3 4 5 6 7 8 9.**

9 pt
The quick brown fox jumps over the lazy dog. 0 1 2 3 4 5 6 7 8 9. *The quick brown fox jumps over the lazy dog. 0 1 2 3 4 5 6 7 8 9.* **The quick brown fox jumps over the lazy dog. 0 1 2 3 4 5 6 7 8 9.**

10 pt
The quick brown fox jumps over the lazy dog. 0 1 2 3 4 5 6 7 8 9. *The quick brown fox jumps over the lazy dog. 0 1 2 3 4 5 6 7 8 9.* **The quick brown fox jumps over the lazy dog. 0 1 2 3 4 5 6 7 8 9.**

12 pt
The quick brown fox jumps over the lazy dog. 0 1 2 3 4 5 6 7 8 9. *The quick brown fox jumps over the lazy dog. 0 1 2 3 4 5 6 7 8 9.* **The quick brown fox jumps over the lazy dog. 0 1 2 3 4 5 6 7 8 9.**

14 pt
The quick brown fox jumps over the lazy dog. 0 1 2 3 4 5 6 7 8 9. *The quick brown fox jumps over the lazy dog. 0 1 2 3 4 5 6 7 8 9.* **The quick brown fox jumps over the lazy dog. 0 1 2 3 4 5 6 7 8 9.**

Black: 50% Tint
HEX #939598

6 pt
The quick brown fox jumps over the lazy dog. 0 1 2 3 4 5 6 7 8 9. *The quick brown fox jumps over the lazy dog. 0 1 2 3 4 5 6 7 8 9.* **The quick brown fox jumps over the lazy dog. 0 1 2 3 4 5 6 7 8 9.**

7 pt
The quick brown fox jumps over the lazy dog. 0 1 2 3 4 5 6 7 8 9. *The quick brown fox jumps over the lazy dog. 0 1 2 3 4 5 6 7 8 9.* **The quick brown fox jumps over the lazy dog. 0 1 2 3 4 5 6 7 8 9.**

8 pt
The quick brown fox jumps over the lazy dog. 0 1 2 3 4 5 6 7 8 9. *The quick brown fox jumps over the lazy dog. 0 1 2 3 4 5 6 7 8 9.* **The quick brown fox jumps over the lazy dog. 0 1 2 3 4 5 6 7 8 9.**

9 pt
The quick brown fox jumps over the lazy dog. 0 1 2 3 4 5 6 7 8 9. *The quick brown fox jumps over the lazy dog. 0 1 2 3 4 5 6 7 8 9.* **The quick brown fox jumps over the lazy dog. 0 1 2 3 4 5 6 7 8 9.**

10 pt
The quick brown fox jumps over the lazy dog. 0 1 2 3 4 5 6 7 8 9. *The quick brown fox jumps over the lazy dog. 0 1 2 3 4 5 6 7 8 9.* **The quick brown fox jumps over the lazy dog. 0 1 2 3 4 5 6 7 8 9.**

12 pt
The quick brown fox jumps over the lazy dog. 0 1 2 3 4 5 6 7 8 9. *The quick brown fox jumps over the lazy dog. 0 1 2 3 4 5 6 7 8 9.* **The quick brown fox jumps over the lazy dog. 0 1 2 3 4 5 6 7 8 9.**

14 pt
The quick brown fox jumps over the lazy dog. 0 1 2 3 4 5 6 7 8 9. *The quick brown fox jumps over the lazy dog. 0 1 2 3 4 5 6 7 8 9.* **The quick brown fox jumps over the lazy dog. 0 1 2 3 4 5 6 7 8 9.**

Black: 25% Tint
HEX #C7C8CA

6 pt
The quick brown fox jumps over the lazy dog. 0 1 2 3 4 5 6 7 8 9. *The quick brown fox jumps over the lazy dog. 0 1 2 3 4 5 6 7 8 9.* **The quick brown fox jumps over the lazy dog. 0 1 2 3 4 5 6 7 8 9.**

7 pt
The quick brown fox jumps over the lazy dog. 0 1 2 3 4 5 6 7 8 9. *The quick brown fox jumps over the lazy dog. 0 1 2 3 4 5 6 7 8 9.* **The quick brown fox jumps over the lazy dog. 0 1 2 3 4 5 6 7 8 9.**

8 pt
The quick brown fox jumps over the lazy dog. 0 1 2 3 4 5 6 7 8 9. *The quick brown fox jumps over the lazy dog. 0 1 2 3 4 5 6 7 8 9.* **The quick brown fox jumps over the lazy dog. 0 1 2 3 4 5 6 7 8 9.**

9 pt
The quick brown fox jumps over the lazy dog. 0 1 2 3 4 5 6 7 8 9. *The quick brown fox jumps over the lazy dog. 0 1 2 3 4 5 6 7 8 9.* **The quick brown fox jumps over the lazy dog. 0 1 2 3 4 5 6 7 8 9.**

10 pt
The quick brown fox jumps over the lazy dog. 0 1 2 3 4 5 6 7 8 9. *The quick brown fox jumps over the lazy dog. 0 1 2 3 4 5 6 7 8 9.* **The quick brown fox jumps over the lazy dog. 0 1 2 3 4 5 6 7 8 9.**

12 pt
The quick brown fox jumps over the lazy dog. 0 1 2 3 4 5 6 7 8 9. *The quick brown fox jumps over the lazy dog. 0 1 2 3 4 5 6 7 8 9.* **The quick brown fox jumps over the lazy dog. 0 1 2 3 4 5 6 7 8 9.**

14 pt
The quick brown fox jumps over the lazy dog. 0 1 2 3 4 5 6 7 8 9. *The quick brown fox jumps over the lazy dog. 0 1 2 3 4 5 6 7 8 9.* **The quick brown fox jumps over the lazy dog. 0 1 2 3 4 5 6 7 8 9.**

Black: 10% Tint
HEX #E6E7E8

6 pt
The quick brown fox jumps over the lazy dog. 0 1 2 3 4 5 6 7 8 9. *The quick brown fox jumps over the lazy dog. 0 1 2 3 4 5 6 7 8 9.* **The quick brown fox jumps over the lazy dog. 0 1 2 3 4 5 6 7 8 9.**

7 pt
The quick brown fox jumps over the lazy dog. 0 1 2 3 4 5 6 7 8 9. *The quick brown fox jumps over the lazy dog. 0 1 2 3 4 5 6 7 8 9.* **The quick brown fox jumps over the lazy dog. 0 1 2 3 4 5 6 7 8 9.**

8 pt
The quick brown fox jumps over the lazy dog. 0 1 2 3 4 5 6 7 8 9. *The quick brown fox jumps over the lazy dog. 0 1 2 3 4 5 6 7 8 9.* **The quick brown fox jumps over the lazy dog. 0 1 2 3 4 5 6 7 8 9.**

9 pt
The quick brown fox jumps over the lazy dog. 0 1 2 3 4 5 6 7 8 9. *The quick brown fox jumps over the lazy dog. 0 1 2 3 4 5 6 7 8 9.* **The quick brown fox jumps over the lazy dog. 0 1 2 3 4 5 6 7 8 9.**

10 pt
The quick brown fox jumps over the lazy dog. 0 1 2 3 4 5 6 7 8 9. *The quick brown fox jumps over the lazy dog. 0 1 2 3 4 5 6 7 8 9.* **The quick brown fox jumps over the lazy dog. 0 1 2 3 4 5 6 7 8 9.**

12 pt
The quick brown fox jumps over the lazy dog. 0 1 2 3 4 5 6 7 8 9. *The quick brown fox jumps over the lazy dog. 0 1 2 3 4 5 6 7 8 9.* **The quick brown fox jumps over the lazy dog. 0 1 2 3 4 5 6 7 8 9.**

14 pt
The quick brown fox jumps over the lazy dog. 0 1 2 3 4 5 6 7 8 9. *The quick brown fox jumps over the lazy dog. 0 1 2 3 4 5 6 7 8 9.* **The quick brown fox jumps over the lazy dog. 0 1 2 3 4 5 6 7 8 9.**

VERDANA

4 pt
The quick brown fox jumps over the lazy dog. 0 1 2 3 4 5 6 7 8 9. *The quick brown fox jumps over the lazy dog. 0 1 2 3 4 5 6 7 8 9.* **The quick brown fox jumps over the lazy dog. 0 1 2 3 4 5 6 7 8 9.**

5 pt
The quick brown fox jumps over the lazy dog. 0 1 2 3 4 5 6 7 8 9. *The quick brown fox jumps over the lazy dog. 0 1 2 3 4 5 6 7 8 9.* **The quick brown fox jumps over the lazy dog. 0 1 2 3 4 5 6 7 8 9.**

6 pt
The quick brown fox jumps over the lazy dog. 0 1 2 3 4 5 6 7 8 9. *The quick brown fox jumps over the lazy dog. 0 1 2 3 4 5 6 7 8 9.* **The quick brown fox jumps over the lazy dog. 0 1 2 3 4 5 6 7 8 9.**

7 pt
The quick brown fox jumps over the lazy dog. 0 1 2 3 4 5 6 7 8 9. *The quick brown fox jumps over the lazy dog. 0 1 2 3 4 5 6 7 8 9.* **The quick brown fox jumps over the lazy dog. 0 1 2 3 4 5 6 7 8 9.**

8 pt
The quick brown fox jumps over the lazy dog. 0 1 2 3 4 5 6 7 8 9. *The quick brown fox jumps over the lazy dog. 0 1 2 3 4 5 6 7 8 9.* **The quick brown fox jumps over the lazy dog. 0 1 2 3 4 5 6 7 8 9.**

9 pt
The quick brown fox jumps over the lazy dog. 0 1 2 3 4 5 6 7 8 9. *The quick brown fox jumps over the lazy dog. 0 1 2 3 4 5 6 7 8 9.* **The quick brown fox jumps over the lazy dog. 0 1 2 3 4 5 6 7 8 9.**

10 pt
The quick brown fox jumps over the lazy dog. 0 1 2 3 4 5 6 7 8 9. *The quick brown fox jumps over the lazy dog. 0 1 2 3 4 5 6 7 8 9.* **The quick brown fox jumps over the lazy dog. 0 1 2 3 4 5 6 7 8 9.**

12 pt
The quick brown fox jumps over the lazy dog. 0 1 2 3 4 5 6 7 8 9. *The quick brown fox jumps over the lazy dog. 0 1 2 3 4 5 6 7 8 9.* **The quick brown fox jumps over the lazy dog. 0 1 2 3 4 5 6 7 8 9.**

14 pt
The quick brown fox jumps over the lazy dog. 0 1 2 3 4 5 6 7 8 9. *The quick brown fox jumps over the lazy dog. 0 1 2 3 4 5 6 7 8 9.* **The quick brown fox jumps over the lazy dog. 0 1 2 3 4 5 6 7 8 9.**

16 pt
The quick brown fox jumps over the lazy dog. 0 1 2 3 4 5 6 7 8 9. *The quick brown fox jumps over the lazy dog. 0 1 2 3 4 5 6 7 8 9.* **The**

quick brown fox jumps over the lazy dog.
0 1 2 3 4 5 6 7 8 9.

18 pt

The quick brown fox jumps over the lazy dog. 0 1 2 3 4 5 6 7 8 9. *The quick brown fox jumps over the lazy dog. 0 1 2 3 4 5 6 7 8 9.* **The quick brown fox jumps over the lazy dog. 0 1 2 3 4 5 6 7 8 9.**

24 pt

The quick brown fox jumps over the lazy dog. 0 1 2 3 4 5 6 7 8 9. *The quick brown fox jumps over the lazy dog. 0 1 2 3 4 5 6 7 8 9.* **The quick brown fox jumps over the lazy dog. 0 1 2 3 4 5 6 7 8 9.**

36 pt

The quick brown fox jumps over the dog. 0 1 2 3 4 5 6 7 8 9. *The quick brown fox*

Black: 75% Tint
HEX #636466

6 pt

The quick brown fox jumps over the lazy dog. 0 1 2 3 4 5 6 7 8 9. *The quick brown fox jumps over the lazy dog. 0 1 2 3 4 5 6 7 8 9.* **The quick brown fox jumps over the lazy dog. 0 1 2 3 4 5 6 7 8 9.**

7 pt

The quick brown fox jumps over the lazy dog. 0 1 2 3 4 5 6 7 8 9. *The quick brown fox jumps over the lazy dog. 0 1 2 3 4 5 6 7 8 9.* **The quick brown fox jumps over the lazy dog. 0 1 2 3 4 5 6 7 8 9.**

8 pt

The quick brown fox jumps over the lazy dog. 0 1 2 3 4 5 6 7 8 9. *The quick brown fox jumps over the lazy dog. 0 1 2 3 4 5 6 7 8 9.* **The quick brown fox jumps over the lazy dog. 0 1 2 3 4 5 6 7 8 9.**

9 pt

The quick brown fox jumps over the lazy dog. 0 1 2 3 4 5 6 7 8 9. *The quick brown fox jumps over the lazy dog. 0 1 2 3 4 5 6 7 8 9.* **The quick brown fox jumps over the lazy dog. 0 1 2 3 4 5 6 7 8 9.**

10 pt

The quick brown fox jumps over the lazy dog. 0 1 2 3 4 5 6 7 8 9. *The quick brown fox jumps over the lazy dog. 0 1 2 3 4 5 6 7 8 9.* **The quick brown fox jumps over the lazy dog. 0 1 2 3 4 5 6 7 8 9.**

12 pt

The quick brown fox jumps over the lazy dog. 0 1 2 3 4 5 6 7 8 9. *The quick brown fox jumps over the lazy dog. 0 1 2 3 4 5 6 7 8 9.* **The quick brown fox jumps over the lazy dog. 0 1 2 3 4 5 6 7 8 9.**

14 pt

The quick brown fox

Black: 50% Tint
HEX #939598

6 pt

The quick brown fox jumps over the lazy dog. 0 1 2 3 4 5 6 7 8 9. *The quick brown fox jumps over the lazy dog. 0 1 2 3 4 5 6 7 8 9.* **The quick brown fox jumps over the lazy dog. 0 1 2 3 4 5 6 7 8 9.**

7 pt

The quick brown fox jumps over the lazy dog. 0 1 2 3 4 5 6 7 8 9. *The quick brown fox jumps over the lazy dog. 0 1 2 3 4 5 6 7 8 9.* **The quick brown fox jumps over the lazy dog. 0 1 2 3 4 5 6 7 8 9.**

8 pt

The quick brown fox jumps over the lazy dog. 0 1 2 3 4 5 6 7 8 9. *The quick brown fox jumps over the lazy dog. 0 1 2 3 4 5 6 7 8 9.* **The quick brown fox jumps over the lazy dog. 0 1 2 3 4 5 6 7 8 9.**

9 pt

The quick brown fox jumps over the lazy dog. 0 1 2 3 4 5 6 7 8 9. *The quick brown fox jumps over the lazy dog. 0 1 2 3 4 5 6 7 8 9.* **The quick brown fox jumps over the lazy dog. 0 1 2 3 4 5 6 7 8 9.**

10 pt

The quick brown fox jumps over the lazy dog. 0 1 2 3 4 5 6 7 8 9. *The quick brown fox jumps over the lazy dog. 0 1 2 3 4 5 6 7 8 9.* **The quick brown fox jumps over the lazy dog. 0 1 2 3 4 5 6 7 8 9.**

12 pt

The quick brown fox jumps over the lazy dog. 0 1 2 3 4 5 6 7 8 9. *The quick brown fox jumps over the lazy dog. 0 1 2 3 4 5 6 7 8 9.* **The quick brown fox jumps over the lazy dog. 0 1 2 3 4 5 6 7 8 9.**

14 pt

The quick brown fox

Black: 25% Tint
HEX #C7C8CA

6 pt
The quick brown fox jumps over the lazy dog. 0 1 2 3 4 5 6 7 8 9. *The quick brown fox jumps over the lazy dog. 0 1 2 3 4 5 6 7 8 9.* **The quick brown fox jumps over the lazy dog. 0 1 2 3 4 5 6 7 8 9.**

7 pt
The quick brown fox jumps over the lazy dog. 0 1 2 3 4 5 6 7 8 9. *The quick brown fox jumps over the lazy dog. 0 1 2 3 4 5 6 7 8 9.* **The quick brown fox jumps over the lazy dog. 0 1 2 3 4 5 6 7 8 9.**

8 pt
The quick brown fox jumps over the lazy dog. 0 1 2 3 4 5 6 7 8 9. *The quick brown fox jumps over the lazy dog. 0 1 2 3 4 5 6 7 8 9.* **The quick brown fox jumps over the lazy dog. 0 1 2 3 4 5 6 7 8 9.**

9 pt
The quick brown fox jumps over the lazy dog. 0 1 2 3 4 5 6 7 8 9. *The quick brown fox jumps over the lazy dog. 0 1 2 3 4 5 6 7 8 9.* **The quick brown fox jumps over the lazy dog. 0 1 2 3 4 5 6 7 8 9.**

10 pt
The quick brown fox jumps over the lazy dog. 0 1 2 3 4 5 6 7 8 9. *The quick brown fox jumps over the lazy dog. 0 1 2 3 4 5 6 7 8 9.* **The quick brown fox jumps over the lazy dog. 0 1 2 3 4 5 6 7 8 9.**

12 pt
The quick brown fox jumps over the lazy dog. 0 1 2 3 4 5 6 7 8 9. *The quick brown fox jumps over the lazy dog. 0 1 2 3 4 5 6 7 8 9.* **The quick brown fox jumps over the lazy dog. 0 1 2 3 4 5 6 7 8 9.**

14 pt
The quick brown fox

Black: 10% Tint
HEX #E6E7E8

6 pt
The quick brown fox jumps over the lazy dog. 0 1 2 3 4 5 6 7 8 9. *The quick brown fox jumps over the lazy dog. 0 1 2 3 4 5 6 7 8 9.* **The quick brown fox jumps over the lazy dog. 0 1 2 3 4 5 6 7 8 9.**

7 pt
The quick brown fox jumps over the lazy dog. 0 1 2 3 4 5 6 7 8 9. *The quick brown fox jumps over the lazy dog. 0 1 2 3 4 5 6 7 8 9.* **The quick brown fox jumps over the lazy dog. 0 1 2 3 4 5 6 7 8 9.**

8 pt
The quick brown fox jumps over the lazy dog. 0 1 2 3 4 5 6 7 8 9. *The quick brown fox jumps over the lazy dog. 0 1 2 3 4 5 6 7 8 9.* **The quick brown fox jumps over the lazy dog. 0 1 2 3 4 5 6 7 8 9.**

9 pt
The quick brown fox jumps over the lazy dog. 0 1 2 3 4 5 6 7 8 9. *The quick brown fox jumps over the lazy dog. 0 1 2 3 4 5 6 7 8 9.* **The quick brown fox jumps over the lazy dog. 0 1 2 3 4 5 6 7 8 9.**

10 pt
The quick brown fox jumps over the lazy dog. 0 1 2 3 4 5 6 7 8 9. *The quick brown fox jumps over the lazy dog. 0 1 2 3 4 5 6 7 8 9.* **The quick brown fox jumps over the lazy dog. 0 1 2 3 4 5 6 7 8 9.**

12 pt
The quick brown fox jumps over the lazy dog. 0 1 2 3 4 5 6 7 8 9. *The quick brown fox jumps over the lazy dog. 0 1 2 3 4 5 6 7 8 9.* **The quick brown fox jumps over the lazy dog. 0 1 2 3 4 5 6 7 8 9.**

14 pt
The quick brown fox

NOTES:

DOTS & DOT GRIDS

Black: 100% Tint; HEX #000000

DOT: 0.01 in
GRID SPACING: 0.1 in

DOT: 0.02 in
GRID SPACING: 0.1 in

DOT: 0.03 in
GRID SPACING: 0.1 in

DOT: 0.01 in
GRID SPACING: 0.2 in

DOT: 0.02 in
GRID SPACING: 0.2 in

DOT: 0.03 in
GRID SPACING: 0.2 in

DOT: 0.01 in
GRID SPACING: 0.3 in

DOT: 0.02 in
GRID SPACING: 0.3 in

DOT: 0.03 in
GRID SPACING: 0.3 in

DOT: 0.04 in
GRID SPACING: 0.1 in

DOT: 0.05 in
GRID SPACING: 0.1 in

DOT: 0.1 in
GRID SPACING: 0.1 in

DOT: 0.04 in
GRID SPACING: 0.2 in

DOT: 0.05 in
GRID SPACING: 0.2 in

DOT: 0.1 in
GRID SPACING: 0.2 in

DOT: 0.04 in
GRID SPACING: 0.3 in

DOT: 0.05 in
GRID SPACING: 0.3 in

DOT: 0.1 in
GRID SPACING: 0.3 in

Black: 75% Tint; HEX #636466

DOT: 0.01 in
GRID SPACING: 0.1 in

DOT: 0.02 in
GRID SPACING: 0.1 in

DOT: 0.03 in
GRID SPACING: 0.1 in

DOT: 0.01 in
GRID SPACING: 0.2 in

DOT: 0.02 in
GRID SPACING: 0.2 in

DOT: 0.03 in
GRID SPACING: 0.2 in

DOT: 0.01 in
GRID SPACING: 0.3 in

DOT: 0.02 in
GRID SPACING: 0.3 in

DOT: 0.03 in
GRID SPACING: 0.3 in

DOT: 0.04 in
GRID SPACING: 0.1 in

DOT: 0.05 in
GRID SPACING: 0.1 in

DOT: 0.1 in
GRID SPACING: 0.1 in

DOT: 0.04 in
GRID SPACING: 0.2 in

DOT: 0.05 in
GRID SPACING: 0.2 in

DOT: 0.1 in
GRID SPACING: 0.2 in

DOT: 0.04 in
GRID SPACING: 0.3 in

DOT: 0.05 in
GRID SPACING: 0.3 in

DOT: 0.1 in
GRID SPACING: 0.3 in

Black: 50% Tint; HEX #939598

DOT: 0.01 in
GRID SPACING: 0.1 in

DOT: 0.02 in
GRID SPACING: 0.1 in

DOT: 0.03 in
GRID SPACING: 0.1 in

DOT: 0.01 in
GRID SPACING: 0.2 in

DOT: 0.02 in
GRID SPACING: 0.2 in

DOT: 0.03 in
GRID SPACING: 0.2 in

DOT: 0.01 in
GRID SPACING: 0.3 in

DOT: 0.02 in
GRID SPACING: 0.3 in

DOT: 0.03 in
GRID SPACING: 0.3 in

DOT: 0.04 in
GRID SPACING: 0.1 in

DOT: 0.05 in
GRID SPACING: 0.1 in

DOT: 0.1 in
GRID SPACING: 0.1 in

DOT: 0.04 in
GRID SPACING: 0.2 in

DOT: 0.05 in
GRID SPACING: 0.2 in

DOT: 0.1 in
GRID SPACING: 0.2 in

DOT: 0.04 in
GRID SPACING: 0.3 in

DOT: 0.05 in
GRID SPACING: 0.3 in

DOT: 0.1 in
GRID SPACING: 0.3 in

Black: 25% Tint; HEX #C7C8CA

DOT: 0.01 in
GRID SPACING: 0.1 in

DOT: 0.02 in
GRID SPACING: 0.1 in

DOT: 0.03 in
GRID SPACING: 0.1 in

DOT: 0.01 in
GRID SPACING: 0.2 in

DOT: 0.02 in
GRID SPACING: 0.2 in

DOT: 0.03 in
GRID SPACING: 0.2 in

DOT: 0.01 in
GRID SPACING: 0.3 in

DOT: 0.02 in
GRID SPACING: 0.3 in

DOT: 0.03 in
GRID SPACING: 0.3 in

DOT: 0.04 in
GRID SPACING: 0.1 in

DOT: 0.05 in
GRID SPACING: 0.1 in

DOT: 0.1 in
GRID SPACING: 0.1 in

DOT: 0.04 in
GRID SPACING: 0.2 in

DOT: 0.05 in
GRID SPACING: 0.2 in

DOT: 0.1 in
GRID SPACING: 0.2 in

DOT: 0.04 in
GRID SPACING: 0.3 in

DOT: 0.05 in
GRID SPACING: 0.3 in

DOT: 0.1 in
GRID SPACING: 0.3 in

Black: 10% Tint; HEX #E6E7E8

DOT: 0.01 in
GRID SPACING: 0.1 in

DOT: 0.02 in
GRID SPACING: 0.1 in

DOT: 0.03 in
GRID SPACING: 0.1 in

DOT: 0.01 in
GRID SPACING: 0.2 in

DOT: 0.02 in
GRID SPACING: 0.2 in

DOT: 0.03 in
GRID SPACING: 0.2 in

DOT: 0.01 in
GRID SPACING: 0.3 in

DOT: 0.02 in
GRID SPACING: 0.3 in

DOT: 0.03 in
GRID SPACING: 0.3 in

DOT: 0.04 in
GRID SPACING: 0.1 in

DOT: 0.05 in
GRID SPACING: 0.1 in

DOT: 0.1 in
GRID SPACING: 0.1 in

DOT: 0.04 in
GRID SPACING: 0.2 in

DOT: 0.05 in
GRID SPACING: 0.2 in

DOT: 0.1 in
GRID SPACING: 0.2 in

DOT: 0.04 in
GRID SPACING: 0.3 in

DOT: 0.05 in
GRID SPACING: 0.3 in

DOT: 0.1 in
GRID SPACING: 0.3 in

OPACITY, GRADIENTS & PHOTOS

OPACITY

#000000	90%	80%	70%	60%
50%	40%	30%	20%	10%

BEHIND BLACK TEXT

#000000	90%	80%	70%	60%

The quick brown fox jumps over the lazy dog. 0 1 2 3 4 5 6 7 8 9. *The quick brown fox jumps over the lazy dog. 0 1 2 3 4 5 6 7 8 9.* **The quick brown fox jumps over the lazy dog. 0 1 2 3 4 5 6 7 8 9.**

50%	40%	30%	20%	10%

The quick brown fox jumps over the lazy dog. 0 1 2 3 4 5 6 7 8 9. *The quick brown fox jumps over the lazy dog. 0 1 2 3 4 5 6 7 8 9.* **The quick brown fox jumps over the lazy dog. 0 1 2 3 4 5 6 7 8 9.**

BEHIND WHITE TEXT

#000000	90%	80%	70%	60%

The quick brown fox jumps over the lazy dog. 0 1 2 3 4 5 6 7 8 9. *The quick brown fox jumps over the lazy dog. 0 1 2 3 4 5 6 7 8 9.* **The quick brown fox jumps over the lazy dog. 0 1 2 3 4 5 6 7 8 9.**

50%	40%	30%	20%	10%

The quick brown fox jumps over the lazy dog. 0 1 2 3 4 5 6 7 8 9. *The quick brown fox jumps over the lazy dog. 0 1 2 3 4 5 6 7 8 9.* **The quick brown fox jumps over the lazy dog. 0 1 2 3 4 5 6 7 8 9.**

GRADIENTS

LINEAR: Black (#000000) to White (#FFFFFF)

RADIAL: Black (#000000) to White (#FFFFFF)

PHOTOS

@bowielafrenchie

5.25 x 7 in

@bowielafrenchie

3 x 4 in

2 x 2.67 in

1 x 1.33 in

0.5 x 0.67 in

NOTES:

NOTES:

NOTES:

Made in the USA
Middletown, DE
26 December 2019